Hiring and Keeping the Best People

The Harvard Business Essentials Series

The Harvard Business Essentials series is designed to provide comprehensive advice, personal coaching, background information, and guidance on the most relevant topics in business. Drawing on rich content from Harvard Business School Publishing and other sources, these concise guides are carefully crafted to provide a highly practical resource for readers with all levels of experience. To assure quality and accuracy, each volume is closely reviewed by a specialized content adviser from a world-class business school. Whether you are a new manager interested in expanding your skills or an experienced executive looking for a personal resource, these solution-oriented books offer reliable answers at your fingertips.

Other books in the series:

Finance
Managing Change and Transition

HARVARD
BUSINESS
ESSENTIALS

Hiring and Keeping the Best People

Harvard Business School Press | *Boston, Massachusetts*

978-1-57851-875-3 (ISBN 13)

Library of Congress Cataloging-in-Publication Data

Harvard business essentials. Hiring and keeping the best people.

p. cm.— (The harvard business essentials series) Includes bibliographical references and index.

ISBN 1-57851-875-X

1. Employee selection. 2. Employee retention. 3. Employee motivation. I. Title: Hiring and keeping the best people. II. Harvard Business School. III. Series.

HF5549.5.S38 H37 2002

658.3'1—dc21

2002010627

Contents

Hiring and Keeping the Best People

Introduction

This book explains the essentials of what managers and business owners need to know about hiring and retaining good employees. Effective hiring and personnel retention are the two bases of future organizational well-being. If that seems like an overstatement, consider this: The success of most of today's businesses depends more on human assets than on physical or financial assets. Buildings, equipment, manufacturing facilities, and most technologies can be readily purchased, but the human talent and know-how needed to drive our knowledge-based industries are much harder to come by.

Hiring decisions are among the most important decisions made by managers, and this book explains the essentials of what managers and business owners need to know about this process. Without the right people in the right positions, neither a company nor its individual units can turn in exceptional performance. Good hiring decisions create a foundation for more effective performance by employees, teams, and the company overall. Conversely, bad hiring decisions drag down performance and are painfully expensive to correct. Bradford Smith, a consultant who helps major corporations with their hiring decisions, has estimated from his study of fifty-four U.S. companies that the average managerial "mis-hire" costs a company *twenty-four times* the individual's base compensation![1] How is that possible? Smith points to all the usual suspects: the mis-hire's compensation and cost of maintenance, the initial hiring cost, severance expenses, the costs associated with hiring and training a replacement, and so forth. But the biggest cost, according to Smith, is the cost of the mistakes, failures, and missed business opportunities

that result from having the wrong person in a management position
over several years. Thus, in his calculation, the average total cost for a
mis-hired manager with a base compensation of $114,000 will cost
a company $2.7 million in not just tangible fees, but the intangible
expenses of errors and lost opportunities.

The damage that mis-hired or mis-placed individuals can cause
is particularly acute when they are managers. C-level managers typically hire C-level players, set lower standards, and eventually create
an exodus of truly competent people. When excellent managers and
great employees are hired, the opposite prevails. Thus, hiring managers have a powerful obligation to their company and to themselves
to treat hiring with the greatest attention and to be as deliberate as
possible in identifying and engaging the best possible people. David
Oglivy summed up the importance of careful hiring when he wrote,
"If each of us hires people who are smaller than we are, we shall
become a company of dwarfs. But if each of us hires people who are
bigger than we are, we shall become a company of giants."

Retention is the other side of the human asset equation. In a
market-driven economy you'll never be able to keep everyone—and
you shouldn't want to. A certain amount of employee turnover can
actually improve the health of an organization, infusing new energy
and new ideas into the ranks. But turnover among valued employees is costly, disruptive, and negatively correlated with customer satisfaction. As this book will reveal, hiring right is a powerful first step
in reducing unwanted turnover. But there are many other things you
can do to make your workplace one that good people will not want
to leave, and these will be addressed here in detail.

What's Ahead

As a manager responsible for hiring decisions, this Harvard Business
Essentials volume will provide you with the basics of hiring and
retaining great people.

Chapter 1 begins with a five-step process for effective hiring,
from determining the job requirements to recruiting, interviewing,
and evaluating candidates, and making an offer.

Chapter 2 digs deeper into key steps of the hiring process. Using a conceptual framework of "embedded life interests," it will help you align individuals with jobs that they will find most satisfying and at which they will excel. The chapter also covers the pros and cons of timely subjects such as online recruiting, the use of "head hunters" and search firms, candidate testing, and the case interview technique.

In Chapter 3, we move from hiring to the field of employee retention. Distilling recent research findings, we will explore why retention matters—as measured by customer satisfaction, turnover costs, and business performance. This chapter explains, in broad strokes, why people stay with a company and why they leave, and points to eight practical steps that managers can take to improve retention.

Chapter 4 looks at the retention challenge from a market perspective. From this perspective, some employees and employee segments represent more value to the organization than others. The market perspective suggests that managers should be less concerned about overall turnover and more concerned with focusing retention attention and resources on those individuals and employee segments that create the most value for the organization. This chapter explains how various market-based strategies can reduce turnover amongst these key individuals and employee segments.

Training and career development are also shown to be effective tools for the retention of valued employees. Chapter 5 describes formal and informal approaches to employee training, explains why training pays, and offers tips on reducing its costs through online learning. In addition to boosting retention, many of your organization's human resource needs can be cultivated internally through employee development—specifically, skill training and career development—and this chapter will also address this key benefit.

The effect of the workplace environment on hiring and retention is the subject of Chapter 6. This chapter not only explains how workplace climate can influence a candidate's decision to take a job and to stick with it, but also addresses how you can alter the culture of your workplace to make it more appealing and to avoid employee burnout. Also discussed are three principles for creating successful work-life balance programs.

Even if you handled every aspect of hiring and retention perfectly, you would still lose some valued employees. This is a fact of life in a free labor market. But as Chapter 7 reveals, the departure of a good employee need not be the end of your productive relationship with that individual. This chapter shows how some professional service firms are using alumni relations programs to keep former employees in their orbits as customers, sources of market intelligence, and, in some cases, as future "rehires." The benefits of rehires, and of using exit interviews to uncover the root causes of employee turnover, are also explored in this final chapter.

In our mission to cover the "essentials" of hiring and retention, we've naturally been able to touch only lightly on many subjects and have left others out entirely. So, for readers who would like to learn more, a number of helpful resources are included at the end of this book: a glossary of terms, an annotated list of relevant articles and books, and three appendices. Appendix A contains a job description that you can use as a model in developing your own descriptions. Appendix B is a generic group of questions that you can use as you interview candidates for just about any type of job. Appendix C describes the "legal landmine" that readers based in the United States need to be aware of, and avoid, in the hiring process.

In addition, you will find invitations throughout the book to visit the official Harvard Business Essentials Web site, www.elearning.hbsp.org/businesstools, for free interactive versions of the tools introduced in this book.

The content in this book is based on a number of books, articles, and online productions of Harvard Business School Publishing, in particular: Peter Cappelli's *Harvard Business Review* article on market-driven retention; various hiring and retention articles published in *Harvard Management Update*; and the hiring module found in Harvard ManageMentor®, an online service.

While this book will help you improve your hiring and employee retention skills, the information given here is of a general nature and is not intended as legal advice nor as a substitute for legal consultation regarding general hiring processes or the management of specific individual situations. With that caveat in mind, let's turn to the five-step hiring process.

1

The Hiring Process

Attracting the Best People

Key Topics Covered in This Chapter

- *Defining job requirements*

- *Recruiting promising candidates*

- *Interviewing*

- *Evaluating candidates*

- *Making the decision and offer*

LIKE MANY OTHER activities undertaken by organizations, hiring is a business process—a set of activities that turn inputs into outputs. This process compiles information about job requirements, the applications of various candidates, and the deliberations of decision makers, and produces an outcome: new people on the payroll. This chapter describes a five-step hiring process. Execute these steps well, and not only will the quality of your hires improve, but you will also be more confident that you are hiring the *right* people.

Defining Job Requirements

Before you can make a good hire, you need to know what you are hiring for. You also need to determine which skills and personal attributes will be a good "fit" with the requirements of the job and the organization.

To define the job and its requirements, you need to understand:

- the primary responsibilities and tasks involved in the job;

- the background characteristics needed to perform the job (education and experience);

- the personal characteristics required (for example, does the individual need to have strong interpersonal skills? Be highly intelligent?);

- the key features of your organization's culture (for example, team-orientation, degree of conformity, reward systems); and

- your managerial style (for example, authoritative, coercive, democratic) and its implications for an effective working relationship.

Primary Responsibilities and Tasks

If you're looking to rehire for an existing job, take a look what the current incumbent is now doing and evaluate their job description, if one exists. But don't simply accept either of these perspectives as definitive. Use the hiring opportunity to reevaluate the primary responsibilities and tasks of the job. Make sure you can answer the question, "What does the employee have to do in this job?"

Education and Experience

Education and experience are the two most critical background characteristics to consider when evaluating candidates. In the case of education, you may wish to specify a certain type of degree or a certain level. Be sure to ask yourself whether a specific educational background is truly necessary. Can you be flexible in this area, or can relevant experience be substituted for a certain educational background?

Experience requirements should be based on a thorough analysis of the specific tasks and responsibilities of the position. Which would be most desirable:

- Industry experience?

- Functional experience?

- Large- versus small-company experience?

Industry and functional experience are particularly important for externally oriented positions requiring knowledge of products and competitors. However, if a good candidate has not been exposed to everything required, consider whether he or she can learn what is needed and how long that learning will take. Various tests, for example, are available to measure an individual's dexterity with numerical data, spatial acumen, mechanical ability, and so forth. Also, determine whether the organization can afford the time needed for on-the-job learning.

Personal Characteristics

Personal characteristics can indicate how the candidate will approach the job and how he or she might relate to coworkers (see "Create Consensus on Personal Characteristics"). Evaluate the following personal characteristics relative to the tasks and responsibilities you've listed for the job opening:

- **Analytical and creative abilities.** A candidate's abilities in these two areas determine how he or she assesses problems and comes up with new approaches to solving them.

- **Decision-making style.** Decision-making style is very individual. Some people are extremely structured, analytical, and fact-based; others rely more on intuition. Some make decisions quickly, while others ponder them for a long time. Some depend on consensus, while others seek their own counsel. It is critical to determine whether a particular style is required for success in the job and, if so, what it is.

- **Interpersonal skills.** Since interpersonal skills and behavior are intimately connected, understanding a candidate's interpersonal skills is an important part of the hiring decision process. To determine which interpersonal skills are most appropriate for a given position, think about the set of tasks that will be performed in the position. Which traits will translate into good performance, especially in view of the superiors, peers, and direct reports with whom the person will interact? For example, a controller should ideally be patient and formal, demonstrating careful, cautious, detail-oriented behavior. For a sales manager, high extroversion and low formality may be desirable.

- **Motivation.** The candidate's personal goals, interests, energy level, and job progression often demonstrate their level of motivation. So ask yourself, "Does this job match the candidate's personal aspirations? Would he or she do the job with enthusiasm and energy?

Develop a Job Description

Once you understand the position's requirements, you are ready to create a job description. A job description is a profile of the job, its essential functions, reporting relationships, hours, and required credentials. This description will make it possible for you to explain the job both to potential candidates and to any recruiters you may be using to help identify candidates. In some cases, your organization may have a required format or a standard job description to use as a model.

A clearly written, results-oriented job description can shape the beginning of the employee relationship, and can help everyone understand the mission, culture, needs, and goals of the company. It can also form the basis of a legal termination of employment should that become necessary. Your job description should include the following:

- job title, business unit, and the name of the organization

- job responsibilities and tasks

- hiring manager and reporting manager

- summary of the job tasks, responsibilities, and objectives

- compensation, hours, and location

- background characteristics required

- personal characteristics required

Many of these items will have to be cleared with the human resource department.

Developing the job description can be an opportunity to redesign a job, instead of just filling the one you already have. For

Create Consensus on Personal Characteristics

Many hiring decisions start off on the wrong foot because the company hasn't clarified exactly what it wants in the new hire. For example, the different people with whom the new hire will interact (or who have a say in the hiring decision) may have their own ideas about the perfect job candidate.

Consider the hypothetical case of a company that wants to fill a product-designer position but hasn't reached a consensus about key hiring factors. The design director wants a seasoned individual who has gained extensive design experience at one of the firm's toughest competitors. The head of finance prefers a bright new (and more affordable) college graduate. The marketing director is pressing for someone with marketing experience in the kinds of product lines the company currently offers. Meanwhile, the new hire's immediate supervisor is looking for someone with "people skills."

Pity the poor job applicant who walks into this situation! To avoid this type of confusion, try this procedure:

- Ask everyone who'll interact with the new hire to privately write down *exactly* what they would consider the attributes of the ideal candidate.

- Meet and openly discuss differences in the various wish lists.

- Decide *together* which requirements have priority.

- Create a new list of requirements that everyone agrees on.

- Stick to that list when evaluating candidates.

example, the last person who held the position may have had a strong strategic focus, but if you decide that a more hands-on manager is now needed, then recreate the job description accordingly. As you go through the exercise of describing the job, observe the following:

- Distinguish between knowledge, skills, and abilities. Some jobs require advanced degrees. Some require special skills, such as knowing how to program in Java. Others require physical abilities, such as hand-eye coordination, or mental abilities, such as the ability to work with numbers. Figure out what you need in each area.

- Take the time needed to do it right. Yes, you need that new employee to start next week, but the cost of getting rid of the wrong employee more than outweighs the cost of time spent finding the right one.

- Be sure to comply with all legal restrictions. Your stated job requirements must be clearly related to getting the job done and must not unfairly prevent racial minorities, women, people with disabilities, or other "protected classes" from getting hired.[1] (U.S. readers should see Appendix C, "Legal Landmines in Hiring.")

For a sample job description, see Appendix A at the end of this book.

Recruiting Promising Candidates

Gaining access to qualified candidates is critical to the success of your hiring effort (see "Tips for Finding the Right Person"). That means creating a pool of qualified applicants. You can accomplish this by getting the word out through as many channels as possible. However, the word "qualified" is important. A large pool of mediocre candidates isn't nearly as valuable as a small pool of *qualified* candidates. Utilizing targeted, relevant channels to get the word out about your position can help ensure that the proportion of qualified candidates in your pool is as high as possible.

Typical channels include recruiting agencies, newspaper ads, referrals from colleagues, trade publications, professional associations, networking, campus recruiting, and the Internet. In addition, you can enhance the pipeline of qualified candidates through programs such as internships and partnerships with colleges, universities, and community organizations.

Personal referrals from current employees are another favored method of expanding the candidate pool, and many companies encourage this through the payment of "rewards" to employees whose referrals are actually hired. In general, this practice is much less costly than others and often produces more satisfactory new hires since it's unlikely that current employees will suggest a candidate who is unqualified or likely to be a bad employee.

Screening Résumés

A sizeable pool of applicants assures that you will have choices in the hiring process; it also means that you'll have more sifting to do in finding the best choice. And that sifting begins with résumé screening (see "Tips for Screening Résumés").

Tips for Finding the Right Person

- Consider current employees.

- Look outside your organization to bring in new outlooks, skills, and experiences.

- Know what kind of person you're looking for in order to locate a good fit.

- Remember that a person's past job performance is the surest guide to future performance.

- Remember that the right education + the right experience + a compatible personality = a good fit.

- Beware of the "just like me" trap. This trap encourages managers to favor candidates who share similar education backgrounds, are of the same age, gender, or race, and who enjoy the same pastimes. To avoid the trap, focus on the objective requirements of the job and the candidate's qualifications.

The cover letter and résumé are the candidate's first introduction to you. In order to merit your further attention, they should convey the qualities you are looking for. When you have a large number of résumés to review, use a two-pass process to make your task more manageable. In the first pass, eliminate the résumés of candidates who do not meet the basic requirements of the job. In the second pass, look for résumés that include:

- signs of achievement and results—for example, a profit orientation, stability, or progressive career momentum;

- a career goal in line with the job being offered (be on your guard here, as applicants are often coached to tailor their purported career goals to match those of jobs to which they're applying); and

- attractive overall construction and appearance.

In this pass, also consider the subtler differences among qualified candidates—for example, years and quality of experience, technical versus managerial backgrounds, the quality of the companies they have worked for in the past, and so forth. Then develop a list of the strongest candidates.

When reviewing résumés, be on the alert for red flags that can indicate areas of weakness such as:

- lengthy description of education (possibly not much job experience);

- employment gaps (what was the applicant doing during these gaps?);

- a pattern of short-term employment, especially after the applicant has been in the work force for more than a few years;

- no logical job progression;

- too much personal information (possibly not much job experience); and

- descriptions of jobs and positions only, with no descriptions of results or accomplishments.

Interviewing

A hiring interview has one primary purpose: To provide both the interviewer and the job candidate with an opportunity to obtain the information they need to make the best possible decision. Since the time spent with any particular job candidate is limited, a well-organized approach helps make the most of that time, yielding more and better information.

When you are selecting someone for an important position, you will probably go through at least two of the following stages for every job opening. In some cases, you may even go through all three.

1. **Telephone-screening interview.** This may be done by you, a recruiting agency, your HR department, or someone else in

Tips for Screening Résumés

- Spend the least amount of your time eliminating the least-likely candidates and the greatest amount of your time carefully considering the most-likely candidates.

- Separate fluff from substance. Get right to the core of the candidate's accomplishments.

- Avoid comparing candidates to each other. Instead, compare each candidate to the high-performer candidate profile and look for a match.

- If you have great numbers of incoming résumés, or tap Internet résumé postings, consider using résumé screening software to automatically identify suitable applicants (more on this in Chapter 2).

your own department. Its purpose is to confirm that the candidate meets the qualifications stated in the ad or other recruiting material, and it can be as short as necessary to accomplish that goal. It is a good opportunity to get some initial impressions of the candidate: Does she call you back at the specified time? Does she communicate well?

2. **Initial in-person interview.** Try to narrow the field to four to seven candidates before holding an initial interview. This interview will probably last 30 to 60 minutes. For less demanding positions, you may find out everything you need to know about the candidate in this interview. Otherwise, you will need to see the person again.

3. **Second interview.** Be very selective about who rates a second interview. At this point, other people with a stake in the process may participate, for example, direct reports, potential peers, or other managers. This interview often brings out more of the "real" person.

Structured versus Unstructured Interviews

In a structured interview, you ask all the candidates the same questions so you can compare answers. Structured interviews are used in order to be fair and objective, but they may not elicit as much information from the candidates. Unstructured interviews are individual conversations that do not necessarily cover all the same questions with every candidate. Instead, they follow lines of inquiry that appear promising. You may learn more about the candidates, but it will be more difficult to compare their responses. And you may miss key information you need in order to make a decision.

It's probably a good idea to steer a middle path between these two approaches—i.e., be flexible in your line of inquiry, but be sure that all interviewees respond to a core set of questions. By preparing those core questions in advance, you can assure yourself and the decision-making team that all key points are covered, and that all candidates respond to them. The unstructured element of the interview opens the door to productive areas of inquiry that neither you nor your colleagues may have anticipated.

Be Prepared

Would you go into a meeting with a vendor to discuss a $500,000 to $1 million custom software package without preparation? Hopefully, you would not. You'd give lots of thought to what you expected the software to do and the features you needed. You'd probably formulate a list of key issues to discuss. Chances are your hiring decisions are costing you something in this same range. So, should you walk into a job interview with notes and prior preparation, or should you simply wing it?

You will gather more of the information you need to make a good hiring decision if you take the time and trouble to prepare. To prepare for a hiring interview, review the job description and make a list of the key responsibilities and tasks of the job, associated training and experience needed, and personal attributes required to do the job well. For each of the areas you need to explore with the candidate, prepare several questions in advance. Figure 1-1, the Interview Preparation Form, is a handy way to organize yourself and gives you something you can take into the interview itself. (For an interactive version of this tool, please visit www. elearning.hbsp.org/businesstools.) For consistency, other interviewers should use the same form but ask their own questions.

There are three phases to the interview: the opening, the body, and the close. Let's consider each in detail.

The Opening

Generally, this should take about 10 percent of the allotted time. Your goal in this phase is to make the candidate feel sufficiently comfortable to open up. There are several things you can do to create this sense of comfort. Be on time. Be friendly. Introduce yourself and tell the candidate something about yourself. Explain the structure of the interview:

FIGURE 1-1

Interview Preparation Form

Job Title:	
Key Responsibilities and Tasks	**Associated Training and/or Experience**
1.	1.
2.	2.
3.	3.
4.	4.
Personal Attributes to Look For:	

Key Areas to Explore	Questions to Ask	Notes
Education	1.	
	2.	
	3.	
Previous Experience	1.	
	2.	
	3.	
Job Accomplishments	1.	
	2.	
	3.	
Skills and Knowledge	1.	
	2.	
	3.	
Personal Attributes	1.	
	2.	
	3.	
Previous Appraisal or Rating	1.	
	2.	
	3.	

Source: HMM Hiring.

"I'm going to ask you about your experience."

"I'm interested in finding out about you as an individual."

"We're interested in finding out whether there is a good fit between your interests and abilities and our organizational needs."

"I will give you information about our organization."

"I'll be glad to take your questions at the end of the interview."

You should also use this interview phase to establish rapport with the candidate. Acknowledge some of the difficulties or awkwardness of being interviewed, such as meeting a lot of new people or being tired at the end of the day. A little humor is generally effective in dispelling the tension that undermines communication. Find information on the résumé that will help you build rapport, or compliment the person on some aspect of his experience. Acknowledge that you have something in common, such as having lived in the same city, a mutual acquaintance, or the same outside interest.

The Body

Plan to use 80 percent of your allotted time in this phase. Use that time to gather the information you will need to evaluate the candidate and to "sell" your organization. During the body of the interview, you need to assess the candidate's qualifications, skills, knowledge, and experience and compare those to the job description you have created. Pursue a direct line of questioning based on the résumé. Identify similarities and patterns of behavior consistent with your ideal profile. Ask for samples of work and references to review after the interview. Samples, if they are not confidential or proprietary, may include a sales brochure, product, customer survey, or training course designed by the candidate. These samples can tell you a great deal about a candidate's capabilities. It is sometimes difficult to get a candidate to be specific about the accomplishments listed on their résumé. But don't allow difficulty to stand between you and the information you require. Remember, a mistake in a hiring decision can be costly and difficult to undo, and enormously expensive if the person is applying for a key decision-making post. So ask directly for details, and probe for tangible measures of success. Table 1-1 provides some examples of typical résumé statements and how you can respond in order to get more detail.

You are also assessing the candidate's personal qualities during this phase, such as leadership, problem-solving ability, communica-

TABLE 1-1

Responses to Typical Résumé Statements

Résumé Statement	Possible Response
I successfully managed development of a new line of consumer kitchenware.	How was success measured: by revenues, time-to-market, other measures? Specifically, what was your role in the development effort?
I worked effectively with marketing and sales to increase annual unit sales by 25 percent over the past twelve months.	What was the nature of your contribution? How were unit sales increased: by more effective selling or by slashing prices?
I initiated the redesign of key department processes.	What processes? What do you mean by "initiated"? Why did you decide to do this? Why was this initiative important?

tion, teamwork skills, and motivation. Use scenario-based questions to determine how people tend to handle situations, such as:

- **For a process manager candidate:** "Suppose that the loan processing department you'd be managing in this position was taking two days more than its competitors to make its decisions and notify customers. How would you approach that type of problem?"

- **For a sales manager candidate:** "Let's say that one of the people in your sales district was well liked by customers and company personnel, had great potential, but wasn't pulling her weight after two years on the job. How would you deal with a situation like that?"

Responses to scenario questions like these will give you an idea about how the candidate approaches problems.

Also, ask the candidate about how he or she handled past situations similar to those he or she would likely encounter as one of your employees: "Tell me about a time when you had to [fire an employee/handle a key customer whose business you'd just lost/lead a process improvement team/etc.]." Be on guard, though, as some people have developed canned responses to some of the more likely scenario-based questions.

Maintaining control of the interview is very important (see "Tips for Conducting the Interview" and "Case Study: A Take-No-Prisoners Interviewer"). The key to maintaining control is to ask most of the questions and do most of the listening. You should be listening 80 percent of the time. You can also maintain control by following a logical line of inquiry. If the candidate strays from this line, return him or her to it.

Be sure to take notes during the interview. Notes will help you recall significant facts about the candidate. But be unobtrusive about it, and tell the candidate up front that you will be taking notes. Remember that your interview notes will become part of the employment file. Avoid writing anything down that could be construed as inconsistent with equal opportunity employment laws.

The Close

Plan on 10 percent of your allotted interview time to wrap things up. The close is your opportunity to:

- Thank the candidate for coming in.

- Explain how and when the person will hear about follow-up interviews or decisions, depending upon your company's policy and your interest in him or her.

- Ask if the candidate has questions, especially those that might affect his or her decision to participate in the next step of the process. If you have reached the interview's time limit, invite the person to call you later with further questions.

- Ask whether there is anything that has not been covered or is unclear.

- Promote your organization. Remember to target the features of your organization that are most likely to appeal to the candidate.

Case Study: A Take-No-Prisoners Interviewer

Brad Smart is an industrial psychologist who specializes in a "chronological in-depth structure" interview, or CIDS, and "topgrading," his term for a lengthy, rigorous executive grading process applied to both incumbent managers and job applicants. As described in a *Fortune* interview, Smart's goal is to identify "A" players, whom he defines as individuals who represent the best-in-class in their job categories.[a] These, he says, are the top 10 percent of the talent available within particular categories.

Smart's interview methodology is more intense than what usually passes for good practice. For example, he asks every serious candidate hundreds of questions about his or her life and career, going back to the person's school years. He inquires about every job and every boss the candidate has had. And to insure that the responses he gets are truthful, Smart lets them know *in advance* that he will speak with every one of the person's bosses over the previous ten years, as well as many of their direct reports. So when he asks them, "What would your former bosses describe as your strengths, weaknesses, and overall performance?" they know they must be absolutely truthful.

Smart was motivated to develop his detailed method by an experience he had observing traditional interviews. As he explained to *Fortune*:

I got an epiphany while working for a human resources management consulting firm 28 years ago. One day my boss asked me to sit in on a job interview to screen a candidate for a client looking to hire a vice president of marketing. I noticed the interview was an hour and a half of general scattergun questions, none of which probed the patterns of how this person developed competencies throughout his career. Things like: "Tell me about yourself" and "How would you handle this?" I immediately saw flaws in the process. Six executives of the client had different opinions about what the job was. They really hadn't analyzed it. I realized most companies hire this way. So I decided to attack the problem.[b]

continued

> Smart estimates that nearly 50 percent of all management-level positions hired through these unsystematic, undisciplined methods are eventually recognized as "mis-hires."

[a] Hank Gilman and Lori Ioannou, "The Smart Way to Hire Superstars," *Fortune,* 10 July 2000, online edition, *www.fortune.com.*
[b] Ibid.

- Shake hands and make eye contact.

- Walk the person to the door or to the next destination.

Some candidates will have questions about salary or benefits at this stage. In some organizations, the human resource department addresses these questions. Others allow the interviewer to disclose the salary or salary range.

Once the candidate has departed, immediately write down any additional notes or observations while they are still fresh in your mind.

Asking Questions

We've already given examples of some typical interview questions. Questions put to the candidate are both a means of controlling the interview and eliciting the information you need to effectively evaluate the prospective employee. It is important to remember, however, that there are good questions, there are aimless questions, and there are outright bad questions. A good question has a purpose, is tied to your decision-making criteria, encourages communication, is job-related, and is nonthreatening. Good questions reflect favorably on you and demonstrate your interest and your preparation. Good questions include:

- Self-appraisal questions that require the candidate to give some thought to his or her interpersonal skills and abilities. These allow the candidate, rather than you, to interpret the facts. (For example: "Why do you think you were selected to lead the task force?")

- Accomplishment questions that ask for evidence of the candidate's demonstrated qualities. They help you learn why and how something was accomplished, and reveal a candidate's level of involvement in past accomplishments. (For example: "Tell me about your contribution to that team effort.")

- Broad-brush questions that make the candidate think about a big topic, choose an answer, and organize his or her thoughts. (For example: "Tell me about your experience as a project manager with the fiber optics group.")

- Comparison questions that reveal a candidate's analytical and reasoning abilities. (For example: "How would you compare working with the fiber optics group to working with the polymer group?")

Bad questions include:

- Leading questions that direct the candidate to the answer you want. (For example: "Would you say you have the motivation required for this job?" Would you expect anyone to say "no" to this?)

- Irrelevant questions that waste everyone's time. (For example, "I see that you are a University of Minnesota alumnus. My daughter may apply there. What are its best programs?")

Appendix B at the end of this book includes suggested interview questions organized around key issues such as the candidate's most recent job, work experience, and skills.

Questions to Avoid

United States laws and regulations are clear about which questions are illegal. If you are not familiar with these laws and regulations,

Tips for Conducting the Interview

- Control the situation. It's your show.

- Don't buy first impressions. Most people make up their minds about an applicant within the first ten minutes. This can be a big mistake. You may miss the real person.

- Help interviewees feel at ease. They'll open up and talk more freely.

- Spend more time listening than talking. Interviewers mistakenly talk about half of the time. Get the candidate to do 80 percent of the talking. The person asking questions and listening is the person who's in control of the interview.

- Have a purpose for every question, otherwise you're wasting valuable time with the applicant—and if that person is a hot commodity, he'll think less of you and your organization.

- Take notes. Put candidates at ease by telling them you will be taking notes before you begin writing.

- Don't make assumptions. Look for repeat patterns of behavior to draw conclusions about the candidate.

- Don't telegraph the right response to the applicant. Author William Swan advises against statements like this one: "[I]t's critical that anyone in this position be able to work on a small project team.... Tell me about your experience and interest in working in such a setting."[a] Ask this question and your applicant will know exactly what you want to hear.

- Be systematic. If you're interviewing several candidates, be sure to query each on the same general set of issues: for example, their backgrounds, what they would bring to the position, their long-term career objectives, and so forth. Their responses to this common set of queries will put you in a better position to compare the candidates.

[a] William S. Swan, *Swan's How to Pick the Right People Program* (New York: John Wiley & Sons, Inc., 1989), 18.

consult your human resources specialist or legal counsel. Prohibited questions in the United State include the following:

How old are you?

Are you married?

What is your citizenship?

What is your sexual orientation?

How much do you weigh?

Are you disabled?

When did you graduate from high school?

Do you have children?

What country are you from?

Where were you born?

Have you ever been arrested?

Would your religion prevent you from working on weekends?

For a more complete discussion of legal and illegal interview questions, see Appendix C, "Legal Landmines in Hiring," at the end of this book.

Evaluating the Candidates

Once you've interviewed all the candidates, you and others involved in the hiring decision must conduct an objective evaluation of each one. A decision-making matrix such as the one shown in figure 1-2 can be a helpful tool for comparing the candidates to one another. (For an interactive version of this tool, please visit *www. elearning.hbsp.org/businesstools*.) Complete this form after you interview each job candidate for a particular position, entering a score for each of the key areas. By tallying the total scores and reviewing your notes from the interviews, you will reduce the chance of making a nonobjective evaluation.

FIGURE 1-2

Decision-Making Matrix

Job Title:

Candidate Name	Key Area Ratings (poor) 1 to 5 (excellent)						
	Education	Previous Experience	Job Accomplish-ments	Skills and Knowledge	Personal Attributes	Previous Appraisal or Rating	TOTAL
	Note:						
	Note:						
	Note:						
	Note:						
	Note:						
	Note:						
	Note:						
	Note:						
	Note:						

Source: HMM Hiring.

Common Evaluation Mistakes

Even though you may take a structured, methodical approach to evaluating your candidates, the evaluation process is still, in the end, subjective. You can neutralize some of that subjectivity by avoiding:

- being overly impressed with maturity or experience, or overly unimpressed by youth and immaturity;

- mistaking a quiet, reserved, or calm demeanor for lack of motivation;

- mistaking the person's ability to play "the interview game," or his or her ability to talk easily, for intelligence or competence;

- allowing personal biases to influence your assessment (for example, you might be tempted to judge someone harshly because she reminds you of someone you dislike);

- looking for a friend or for a reflection of yourself in the candidate;

- assuming that graduates of certain institutions or employees of certain organizations are automatically better qualified;

- giving too much weight to familiarity with the jargon of your business;

- focusing only on one or two key strengths and overlooking the absence of others; and

- failing to value motivation to get ahead.

References Checks

Reference checks verify claims made by the candidate during the interview process and fill in information gaps. They can also provide valuable outside perspectives on the candidate and his or her potential fit with the position. Check references when you are near the end of your recruiting process and close to making a decision. But be sure to obtain permission from the candidates first to avoid affecting someone's current employment—for example, the applicant's company may have no idea that he or she is interviewing for a job elsewhere.

In checking references you have two aims. The first is to verify what the applicant has told you about his or her work experience: where, how long, last position held, and particular assignments. The second aim is learn about the applicant's successes and failures, work habits, strengths and weaknesses, and so forth.

The business of reference checking is critically important since it helps assure the hiring company that the job candidate has truthfully represented his position, work experience, and accomplishments. The comments of a reference can also provide another slant on the candidate's persona. Unfortunately, particularly in the United States, many companies are wary of saying much of anything about a current or former employee for fear of being sued for libel or slander if the employee fails to get a job because of something they said. So getting straightforward comments from some references may be difficult.

Here are some tips for checking references:

- Use the telephone to check references. Since nothing is written down, a person who might be wary of being sued for saying something negative about the applicant is more likely to give you a candid response. Don't check references via letter; you probably won't get much information.

- Take a little time to build rapport with the reference; that will make him or her more comfortable with sharing information with you.

- Briefly describe the job that the candidate is applying for and ask if this is something for which the person would be well suited.

- Ask about the candidate's style, character, strengths, and weaknesses.

- Avoid asking vague questions, such as: "Did Jack do a good job managing his department?" Instead, ask more specific questions, such as: "What was Jack best at?"; "What did his subordinates like best about him?"; "What did they like least?"; "Are there any jobs that would be inappropriate for Jack?"; "What kind of organizational environment would suit Jack best?"

- Let one reference lead to another. If a reference gives you some information, ask, "Do you know anyone who could tell me about Jack's experience in this area?" The more people you talk to, the clearer a picture you will get.

Many people find reference checking a distasteful chore and give the task limited attention. Checking references for candidates "is about as appetizing as eating fish eyes," says Pierre Mornell.[2] But the stakes are so high that you must make the effort and be persistent in digging out the information—even though people may be unwilling to share it. In his book, *Hiring Smart!,* Mornell offers this fast and legal hint for reference checking:

Call references at what you assume will be their lunchtime—you want to reach an assistant or voice mail. If it's voice mail, leave this simple message. If it's an assistant, be sure that he or she understands the last sentence of your message. You say "John (or Jane) Jones is a candidate for (the position) in our company. Your name has been given as a reference. Please call me back if the candidate was outstanding."[3]

The results, says Mornell, are both immediate and revealing. "If the candidate is outstanding or excellent, I guarantee that eight out of ten people will respond quickly and want to help." In contrast, if very few or no references return your call, their silence speaks volumes about the candidate without making any derogatory or libelous statements.

Making the Decision and Offer

Résumés, interviews, and reference checks all inform the decision-making process. At some point, you must ask yourself, "Do we have enough information to make a good decision?" If the answer is "yes," then it's time to move ahead with making the hiring decision.

Rank your top three candidates, and then ask this question of each: "Do we want this person to work for us?" Remember that the goal of the hiring process is not to simply choose the "most qualified" of the existing applicants, but to hire a person who can help the organization meet its objectives (see "Avoid These Two Hiring Mistakes").

Once you've answered both questions affirmatively, make an offer to the candidate who is most able and most likely to help your company meet its goals. If you do not have sufficient information to make a good decision, then determine exactly what additional information you and your colleagues need, how you will obtain it, and what uncertainties you can reasonably expect to reduce. To reduce important uncertainties you may need to call a candidate back for yet another interview, or you may need to do more reference checking.

The Job Offer

Be sure that you understand your organization's policy on who makes the job offer. In some organizations, the immediate supervisor or manager makes the offer. In others, it's the job of the human resource department.

Job offers are usually made in person or by telephone. After extending a verbal offer, you should also send a written confirmation. In both cases, make the offer with enthusiasm and a personal touch, perhaps by referring to something positive that you recall from the interview. Even as you make the offer, continue to gather information from the candidate regarding his or her concerns, the timing of the decision, and other organizations he or she may be considering.

The Offer Letter

An offer letter is an official document, so be sure to seek advice from the appropriate channels before sending it. Do *not* imply that the offer is an employment contract. Include important facts in the letter, such as:

Avoid These Two Hiring Mistakes

Watch out for these commonly made mistakes when you make your hiring choices:

Desperately seeking the "hottest" prospects. Don't assume that that your firm has to hire the hottest, best, and brightest job candidates on the market. Why not?

- Winning them may cost your firm more than it can comfortably afford.

- Their educational or professional background may be more than what the job in question actually requires.

- They may be so confident of their desirability that they won't bring a healthy dose of appreciation and gratitude to their new job at *your* firm—and they'll always have one eye out for the "bigger, better deal."

Hiring in your own image. Another all-too-common mistake is to hire people who are just like you. Many managers assume that they can build strong departments or teams by gathering people who all have the same strengths and personalities—those defined by the managers themselves. But remember: Diversity in personality, work styles, and decision-making approaches

- creates richness in a department's or team's culture,

- increases the group's chances of generating creative ideas and solutions, and

- lets members complement one another's strengths *and* make up for one another's weaknesses.

- starting date

- job title

- expected responsibilities

- compensation

- benefits summary

- time limit for responding to the offer

Don't Forget Process Improvement

This chapter has described hiring as a process with a number of identifiable steps. In this sense hiring is similar to other business processes: billing, order fulfillment, manufacturing, customer service, and so forth.

Like other processes, hiring should be the focus of continual improvement. Every major hiring experience should be followed by a postmortem in which participants evaluate the effectiveness of each process step, pinpoint weaknesses and seek their root causes, and identify opportunities for improvement. The individuals involved in hiring should ask:

- How effective is our approach to defining job requirements? Are the right people in the company involved? Are we more concerned with how the job *has been* designed than with how it *should be* designed?

- Is our current mix of recruiting methods producing an attractive mix of candidates? If it isn't, what can we do to attract more and better-qualified candidates?

- Is our method of screening applicants efficient and effective? What are best practices in this area?

- Does our interview process produce the information we need to make good hiring decisions? Is there consistent quality across interviewers and interview sessions? Do some interviewers need more training?

- Is our candidate evaluation process objective, rigorous, and consistent? How could we make it better?

- When we make a job offer, is the offer clear and compelling? When we strike out with a job offer, do we find out why our offer was rejected?

When an effort is made to improve the hiring process, the quality of your hires will likewise improve.

Summing Up

This chapter has described hiring as a process with a number of key steps:

- **Defining job requirements.** You have to know very clearly what you're hiring for, and the package of skills, experience, attitude, and personal characteristics that you and other people involved in the hiring process require.

- **Recruiting.** This step involves casting your net strategically in order to create a pool of qualified candidates. Screening résumés is part of this step.

- **Interviewing.** The interview process aims to provide both the interviewer and the job candidate with an opportunity to obtain the information they need to make the best possible decision. The best interviews have a core of questions asked to all candidates, and these provide a common base of comparison and evaluation later.

- **Evaluating the candidates.** Once all candidates have been interviewed, the people involved in the hiring decision must conduct an objective evaluation of each. Here, a decision-making matrix can help to organize the interview notes and recollections of many people.

- **Making a decision and offer.** The last step of the hiring process is making the decision and extending a job offer. Always aim for the individual who can contribute the most to your organization's success.

Like any process, hiring is amenable to continual improvement. You and the organization as a whole can become more effective at hiring if you treat each encounter as a learning experience. Reflect on what you did well and what you did poorly. Then incorporate that learning into your next hiring experience.

2

Beyond the Hiring Basics

Details You Need to Know

Key Topics Covered in This Chapter

- *Recruiting online*

- *Deciding when to use a professional recruiter*

- *Using the "case" interview technique*

- *Identifying "embedded personal interests" in order to evaluate candidates*

- *The importance of organizational culture in matching people to jobs*

- *The pros and cons of psychological testing for candidates*

THE PREVIOUS CHAPTER described several key steps in the hiring process. This chapter will dig more deeply into three of those steps: recruiting, interviewing, and evaluating candidates. In further exploring the recruiting step, we will examine the recruiting opportunities offered by the Internet and by professional search firms. We will next examine the application of the "case" interview technique in the interviewing process. Lastly, we will delve into the process of evaluating how well a person will fit into a job and the work environment through an examination of "embedded personal interests," microculture compatibility, and psychological testing of candidates.

Online Recruiting

The Internet is transforming corporate recruiting.[1] Monster.com alone hosts 18 million résumés (13 percent of the U.S. labor force), and on any given day, several million people are busily combing its site. And Monster.com is not alone; there are now thousands of Web sites offering job listings.

Some 90 percent of U.S. companies now recruit online—and for very hardheaded reasons. Online recruiting lets firms target many qualified candidates for a job, screen them in seconds, and contact the best ones immediately. It is only one-twentieth the cost of want ad hiring and slices fifteen days off the usual forty-three day hiring cycle.

The Web allows managers to reach larger numbers of potential candidates, and in venues that weren't available in the past. It also allows companies to pinpoint their recruiting efforts and to set themselves apart from competitors through creative electronic tactics. But companies that use the Internet solely as an extension of paper-based recruiting practices fail to exploit the power of the new medium. Here are some tips—and some cautions:

1. **Broaden the pool of candidates.** In a drum-tight labor market, companies must use the Internet to reach both "active" and "passive" candidates. Active candidates are those who post their résumés on online job boards. Passive candidates—qualified workers happily employed elsewhere—make up a larger and more appealing pool.

   To reach passive candidates, some experts recommend that one or more HR personnel be dedicated to visiting and searching through the Web sites frequented by prime candidates. For example, if your company needs Java programmers, consider their probable age and preferences. Mostly between twenty-two and twenty-nine years old, they surf the Web heavily and are likely to visit several sites for information on Java—JavaWorld.com, *Java Developer's Journal*.www.javadevelopersjournal.com/java), and Gamelan.com. These same people might check CN@Pnet.com for technology news, CNet.com for technology reviews, Tunes.com for music downloads and purchases, ESPN.com for sports, and CNN.com for news. Every one of these URLs accepts banner advertisements—banners that could be used to recruit candidates who hadn't given much thought to leaving their current jobs.

2. **Focus on the best sources.** One lesson people are learning as they pursue online recruiting is that simply posting job openings on your company Web site or on big commercial boards, such as Monster.com, Hotjobs.com, or Career-Path.com, is unlikely to yield the right candidates quickly—or at all. The reason is that your message is likely to be lost in the crowd. One way to boost the odds of success is to target smaller sites—

specifically, the increasing number of Web sites that focus on particular types of jobs in specific locales. Careers.wsj.com, for example, positions itself as the number-one site for mid- to senior-level executives.

For technical personnel, many recruiters are unaware of the existence of Usenet, a global system of discussion groups. Its bulletin boards can be extremely specific regarding job function and location (for example, fl.jobs.computers.programming lists only job openings in Florida for computer programmers). A moderator even ensures that job postings meet site criteria.

3. **Set yourself apart.** When talent is in short supply, an employer must adapt marketing logic to its recruiting effort. In effect, it must approach qualified potential recruits as "customers." And the first step in marketing is differentiation.

Employers are coming up with clever uses of the Internet to differentiate themselves from competitors. Some companies add a link to Datamasters.com on their Web sites, encouraging potential applicants in other regions to compare costs of living and to estimate relocation costs. Others sport résumé builders on their sites. Caterpillar, for example, offers a fill-in-the-blank résumé form on its site (www.cat.com) that encourages applicants to file on the spot rather than go through the more complicated process of writing, printing, and mailing a traditional résumé and cover letter. The form also allows Caterpillar to specify the information it wants from job seekers by inserting, for example, a field for "technical, manufacturing, or computer-based skills." A regularly updated list of available positions at Caterpillar, sorted by location, function, and division, is linked to the résumé-building page. One enterprising company, an IT marketing agency in New York City, went so far as to install a Web camera in its offices so that potential recruits could get a look at the company's creative workspace.

4. **Use recruiting software to avoid being drowned in data.** Lacking an effective filtering mechanism, your recruiters could easily be overwhelmed by the résumés found on the Web or

e-mailed directly to them. Fortunately, several companies have developed recruiting software that allows companies to search the Web and download relevant prospects to a database, where they can be managed and evaluated. Thanks to this type of software, recruiters and HR personnel can spend more time posting jobs, reviewing online résumés, and matching up applicants with specific positions, rather than slogging through irrelevant material.

Keep Web Hiring in Perspective

Although two to three million résumés are posted online today, remember that this is a small fraction of the 140 million people in the American labor force. So, from the recruiting company's viewpoint, it may be seeing just a small fraction of qualified individuals in its search. And in terms of individuals picking up your company on their radar, the numbers are not entirely encouraging either. Market research firm Odyssey, in San Francisco, estimates that only 12 percent of the 102 million households in the United States include anyone who has hunted for a job online. Nevertheless, many of the "right" people from your recruitment perspective may have posted their résumé online. And as more companies and individuals get onboard, the online recruiting proportions will become more favorable.

In terms of quality of recruits, remember that online recruiting is a broadly cast net. Unlike job postings in targeted trade publications, online postings are available to all, regardless of qualifications. Thus, a posting on one of the mega job sites might yield little more than a pile of résumés that will take you hours and hours to screen. This reality underscores the fact that the best source of good people is often referrals from your current employees.

Four Steps

Peter Cappelli, a professor at The Wharton School, advocates a four-step approach to online recruiting:[2]

Step 1. Attract candidates. Many applicants choose potential employers based on the firm's image. Consequently, Cappelli urges companies to integrate their recruiting efforts with their other marketing campaigns. Here are some tips for that integration and for generating a broader pool of candidates:

- Build a recognizable brand by using a recognizable "look" in both recruiting *and* product ads.
- Design your Web page to woo potential recruits: Cite workplace awards you've received (for example, *Fortune's* "100 Best Companies to Work For") and highlight links to information about your firm's perks and values.
- Encourage employees to e-mail job ads to qualified friends.

Step 2. Sort applicants. Online recruiting can produce a huge number of résumés. The challenge is to sort through these quickly without tossing out the choice candidates. Per Cappelli's findings, here are some solutions:

- Electronically screen applicants with simple online questions, such as, "Are you willing to relocate?" or "When could you start work?" Questions like these can screen out the obvious mismatches. (See "A Legal Caveat" for more about screening questions.)
- Use online tests and games to elicit information about applicants' interests, attitudes, and abilities.

Step 3. Make contact. Online recruiting operates in a different time frame than that to which traditional HR departments are accustomed. It's very fast! Recruiters not only must recognize this different pace, but must adapt to it. Cappelli offers a few tips for doing this:

- Connect a "live" person with a desirable applicant immediately.
- Get your recruiters to think and act like entrepreneurs. Thus, it may be advisable to take online recruiting out of the hands of old-line HR managers, who may be unused to moving quickly.

- Give line managers a larger say in hiring. Decentralization allows candidate-seeking business units to go directly to online job boards to seek their own candidates.

Step 4. Close the deal. Once you've made contact, the Internet connection should move to the background, and good old-fashioned person-to-person contacts should move front and center. In this step, the people doing the hiring need to concentrate on the traditional business of getting to know potential hires and acquainting them with the organization. If they don't, too many good applicants will slip through their fingers.

Recruiters in this stage should build personal relationships with candidates and let the best of those candidates know that they are wanted. To assure that this happens, one expert cited by Cappelli advocates that recruiters spend only one hour per day on the Web, and the rest of their time in personal contact with qualified candidates. Others suggest that one group of recruiters concentrates on finding qualified people and another handles offline interactions.

A Legal Caveat

Antidiscrimination regulations are as big a minefield for online recruiters as they are for traditional recruiters. Thus, if you "screen" online applicants with particular questions, psychological tests, or credit checks you must be sure that these screening elements are job-related—and you must be prepared to prove it! (More about this under "Personality Testing.")

Outsourcing online recruiting to an independent vendor does not let you off the hook. In the United States, courts have held firms liable for antidiscrimination violations resulting from their vendors' screening techniques.

When to Use a Professional Recruiter

Rapid economic growth and high employee turnover over the last decade have created a minor industry out of matchmaking between companies and job seekers. These "matchmakers" go by various names, including employment agencies, technical recruiters, and executive search firms (or "head-hunters"). Some are very generalized while others specialize in particular fields, such as accounting, information technology, or pharmaceuticals. Most charge on a contingency basis—that is, they only get paid if an individual is hired. Payment is generally about 30 percent of the new hire's first year compensation. Those engaged directly by firms to round up a handful of qualified candidates—particularly for senior management posts—charge a nonrefundable retainer, or a contingency fee, and expect to be reimbursed for their expenses. So the costs add up.

Used effectively, these recruiting companies can save you the time and expense you would otherwise expend in generating and initially screening your own pool of qualified job candidates. And in many cases they do a better job of it. For example, specialized firms generally have very active networks of key people in the industries they serve. If you have a notable vacancy—say for a vice president of business development—head-hunters will get the word out quickly and confidentially to qualified people who would otherwise never know of your vacancy. They also screen respondents so that only qualified candidates are presented for evaluation. Lastly, they can do some of the negotiating that might sour an eventual company-employee relationship. You must determine, however, whether their services are worth the cost.

Obviously, you don't have to enlist professional services when your board is acquainted with the right external candidates or when it plans to hire from within. In his advice to readers of the *Harvard Business Review*, Claudio Fernández-Araóz, himself an executive search professional, cites other instances when these services are not needed:[3]

- when the candidate pool is small and known to management

- when the requirements of the open position and the competencies of the successful candidate are clear

- when the position seeking to be filled is highly technical and demands very specialized knowledge and expertise (those hard competencies, per Fernández-Araóz, are easier to evaluate than "soft" managerial and leadership abilities)

- when it is a low-level position

But he makes a case for calling in a professional search firm in many other situations. The first is when a company is hiring for a very high-level position that has a great impact on the bottom line. "Even if an executive search firm finds a candidate who generates only 1% more profits than an alternative candidate does," he says, "it has paid for itself many times over. Moreover, professional firms are often better than in-house staff at conducting the fast and confidential searches often required in high-level situations."[4]

Outside help also makes sense when diversification or joint ventures create new job categories that the hiring organization doesn't really understand, or when it needs to bring in someone from another industry with skills the hiring company lacks. Fernández-Araóz cites the case of a stodgy investment company that decided to look for a new marketing director with experience in consumer product branding—something quite foreign (at the time) to investment marketers. Its search firm had experience in that area and quickly generated a list of excellent candidates from the automobile, breakfast cereal, and clothing industries. "The company ended up hiring the breakfast cereal marketing executive, who did indeed rejuvenate the company's brand," writes Fernández-Araóz.

Turning over the job to a head-hunter doesn't mean that the hiring company and its executives can detach themselves from responsibility. They must stay involved. Fernández-Araóz's advice for staying involved is to:

- **Select a consultant, not just a firm.** Hire the consultant as you would a job candidate, through interviews with the person responsible for the search, and check references from past clients. How happy were they with his or her services? And since no one can do the entire job alone, try to ascertain something about the consultant's supporting staff and their stability as a team. Will that team stay intact while it's working for you?

- **Be aware of potential conflicts of interest.** A commission-paid search firm usually doesn't get paid if the winning candidate is a current employee. That may influence the search firm to exclude your personnel from the pool of candidates, even though their job is to find you the best candidate. A fee-based compensation plan can eliminate this type of conflict.

- **Work as a team.** Finally, Fernández-Araóz advocates teamwork between the hiring company and the search firm. "Your full involvement is critical," he says, "starting with the problem definition, through the homework stage, and into the final offer. While consultants can add value throughout this process, nobody knows the job and the organization better than its own executives."[5]

Case Interviewing

General guidelines for conducting a hiring interview were offered in the previous chapter. Following those guidelines will help you get an accurate fix on the job candidate. Having many people interview the candidate and ask questions from their individual perspectives can improve accuracy even more. Some companies go further, employing "case interviewing" to get a deeper understanding of the applicant and how he or she approaches problems.

Case interviewing is a method that subjects a job applicant to a scenario and business problem similar to those encountered on the job. The candidate is expected to respond with one or more well-reasoned solutions to the problem. For example, in a case designed for evaluating a marketing manager candidate, the interviewer might describe the general characteristics of an industry and its customer market and then ask the candidate what strategy he or she would use to establish a new product line in that market. The candidate's description would reveal something about the candidate's ability to deal with ambiguity, identify possible solutions, and organize his or her thinking on strategic questions.

Management consulting firms, which are continually recruiting new members (the typical turnover rate in that industry is around 22 percent) have used the case interviewing method for many years, and for obvious reasons. They need people who can develop a strategic viewpoint. Other leading firms have picked up the technique—Frito-Lay, Johnson & Johnson, Kraft, Microsoft, Staples, and Dell among them. As cited in a *Harvard Management Update* article on this subject, a Staples manager said that: "Case interviewing enables us to see first-hand how a candidate tackles a strategic question and communicates possible solutions . . . . It also pinpoints those who can see the big picture."[6]

According to Melissa Raffoni, author of that article, case interviewing has traditionally focused on testing problem-solving abilities. Interviewers who use it can observe how candidates approach a problem, the logic they apply, and their choice of questions. However, she notes that interviewers can also test job-specific skills: for example, by asking candidates for market management jobs how they would approach pricing and sales forecasting. According to Raffoni, the power of case interviewing is threefold:

> 1. *It gets as close to real-life situations as possible. It's a chance to see someone's mind work with little or no preparation. This allows you to evaluate interviewees who have well-polished answers to conventional questions such as "Where do you want to be in five years?"*
>
> 2. *It helps candidates gain a better understanding of the job. I have had many candidates end a case and say, "I was a little unclear about the job before the interview; this gave me a better sense of what's involved."*

3. It tests a variety of skills. Case interviewing can test competencies such as strategic thinking, analytical ability, and judgment, along with a variety of communication skills, including active listening, questioning, and dealing with confrontation. Particularly for positions where there is no "right" background or "typical" candidate—that is, no requirement for specific degrees or experience—case interviewing allows you to put everyone on the same footing.[7]

The case interviewing technique has some drawbacks. For starters, it requires substantial time, perhaps more than a company has available. This argues in favor of applying case interviewing to higher-level applicants only. It also favors individuals who are naturally "fast on their feet" over others who process and respond to information in different ways. Nor is this method useful in testing motivation, leadership, or a person's ability to work with others. For these reasons, Raffoni urges that case interviewing be used in conjunction with traditional methods.

Hiring Based on Embedded Personal Interests

The previous chapter discussed the importance of identifying the "personal characteristics" that a candidate needs to possess in order to fulfill the requirements of any given job—characteristics such as motivation, intelligence, and interpersonal skills. People who are deeply and passionately interested in the activities that define their jobs, and are more skilled at executing them, are more likely to be successful in their work. Therefore we will explore the important role of personal characteristics here in more depth.

Based on interviews with some 650 professionals in many industries over a ten-year period, psychologists Timothy Butler and James Waldroop developed a conceptual framework that outlines eight "embedded life interests" through which people generally find personal expression:[8]

1. application of technology

2. quantitative analysis

3. theory development and conceptual thinking

4. creative production

5. counseling and mentoring

6. managing people and relationships

7. enterprise control

8. influence through language and ideas

These core interests are grouped into three main categories in tables 2-1, 2-2, and 2-3: application of expertise, working with people, and control and influence. Since these interests can be very useful in evaluating the "fit" between job candidates and the positions they aspire to, let's consider each of them in turn.

Application of Technology

People with a life interest in the application of technology are intrigued by how things work and are curious about finding better ways to use technology to solve business problems. As Butler and Waldroop write, "People with [this] life interest often enjoy work that involves planning and analyzing production and operations systems and redesigning business processes."[9] They cite the example of a money manager who acts as his company's unofficial computer consultant because he loves the challenge of this type of work more than he does his regular job.

How do you spot people with this interest? See who gets excited when plans are hatched for a new computer system or a process reengineering project.

Quantitative Analysis

"Some people aren't just good at running the numbers, they excel at it. They see it as the best, and sometimes the only, way to figure out business solutions. Similarly, they see mathematical work as fun . . . . Not all 'quant jocks' are in jobs that reflect that deeply embedded life interest," write Butler and Waldroop. In fact, more than a few find themselves in other kinds of work for the wrong reason: because

TABLE 2-1

Category 1: Application of Expertise

Application of Technology	Quantitative Analysis
Examples:	*Examples:*
• engineering	• market research
• computer programming	• forecasting
• production and systems planning	• cash-flow analysis
• product and process design	• computer-model building
• process analysis	• production scheduling
• production planning	• investment analysis
• systems analysis	• accounting
• mechanical crafting/manufacturing	
• researching	

Theory Development and Conceptual Thinking	Creative Production
Examples:	*Examples:*
• economic-theory developing	• new-product designing
• business-model developing	• marketing and advertising
• competition analysis	• developing innovative approaches and solutions
• designing "big-picture" strategy	• event planning
• process designing	• conducting public relations
• teaching business theory	• entertaining
	• writing
	• illustrating

they were told that following their true passion would narrow their career prospects.

To identify people with this particular interest, look for individuals who are intrigued by cash-flow analysis, methods for forecasting sales, and other numbers-based activities. If a market manager is more

TABLE 2-2

Category 2: Working with People

Counseling and Mentoring	Managing People and Relationships
Examples:	*Examples:*
• coaching	• managing others to accomplish business goals
• training	• directing
• teaching	• supervising
• helping	• leading and inspiring others
• drawing people out	• selling
• supporting	• negotiating
• providing feedback and advice	• motivating

interested in the analysis of customer data than in what's said in a customer focus group, he's probably a quantitative analysis person.

Theory Development and Conceptual Thinking

"For some people, nothing brings more enjoyment than thinking and talking about abstract ideas," say Butler and Waldroop. "People with this interest can be excited by building business models that explain competition within a given industry or by analyzing the competitive position of a business with a particular market."

To spot a theory and concept person, look for someone who could easily have followed an academic career, who subscribes to academic publications, and who enjoys conversations about abstract concepts.

Creative Production

These people are imaginative, "out-of-the-box" thinkers. They are comfortable and engaged during brainstorming sessions. Write Butler and Waldroop, "[M]any entrepreneurs, R&D scientists, and engineers have this life interest. Many of them have an interest in the

TABLE 2-3

Category 3: Control and Influence

Enterprise Control	Influence through Language and Ideas
Examples:	Examples:
• controlling resources to actualize a business vision	• negotiating
	• deal making
• setting strategic direction for a company, business unit, work team, or division	• conducting public relations
• having ultimate decision-making authority	• selling
	• persuading
• making deals	• designing advertising campaigns
• holding ultimate responsibility for business transactions, such as trades, sales, and so on	• communicating ideas through writing or speaking

arts. . . . Many people with this interest gravitate toward creative industries such as entertainment."

These individuals, say the authors, are easy to identify. Unconventional clothing is a giveaway. Also, they are less interested in the features of current products than in whatever is *new*.

Counseling and Mentoring

Individuals bitten by this bug like to teach. In business, teaching takes the forms of coaching and mentoring. Many like feeling useful to others; some genuinely take satisfaction from the success of those they counsel. To spot a counselor/mentor, simply observe how they interact with their direct reports.

Managing People and Relationships

Individuals with this life interest enjoy dealing with people on a day-to-day basis. They derive satisfaction from workplace relationships, but they focus much more on outcomes than do people in counseling/mentoring category.

For this life interest, look for people who like to motivate, organize, and direct others.

Enterprise Control

These are the people who like to be in charge, whether it's their high school class or a division of a corporation. They are happiest when they have decision-making authority over their little piece of the universe. How do you spot them? Per Butler and Waldroop: "These individuals . . . ask for as much responsibility as possible in any work situation. . . . A person with this life interest wants to be the CEO, not the COO."

Influence through Language and Ideas

These people enjoy storytelling, negotiating, and persuading. They are most fulfilled through writing, speaking, or both, and are often drawn to careers—such as public relations, journalism, and advertising—where these are viewed as regular and important skills.

These people tend to be the volunteers who write up the project proposal or make the new product presentation to the company sales force.

Because many people have more than one interest, these categories of life interests may overlap in an individual. For example, a financial manager who enjoys using her special quantitative skills may be a very good "people person" and want to work with marketing personnel. So don't try to pigeonhole individuals too narrowly.

Hiring primarily for interests is far more potent than hiring for skills and values for several reasons:

- A job that satisfies someone's deepest interests will keep that person's attention and inspire him or her to perform and achieve. For example, Sarah had no formal training in biology or environmental science, yet her passion for bird–watching led through several levels of self-study and field experience. Initially hired as an intern by a state chapter of a major environmental organization, she eventually rose to the rank of Chief Ornithologist.

- A person may be good at a particular job (that is, possess the perfect skills), but if the job doesn't let that individual express core interests, he or she won't be happy with the work for long. For example, Phil earned his Ph.D. in chemistry and took a job in the R&D unit of a global chemical firm. As a bench scientist, he did an outstanding job and earned regular promotions. So when Phil quit his job to take a management position with another company, his boss was very surprised. When asked why he had made this choice, Phil replied: "I'm really not that interested in science."

- It's far easier to help someone acquire or strengthen skills than to make that person feel an enduring passion for his or her work.

Certainly, skills play an important role in matching the right person to the right job. And new hires must have enough of the appropriate background, experience, and ability to perform well on the job fairly quickly. Nevertheless, a perfect "interests match" increases the likelihood that the employee will stay with the company more than a perfect "skills match" will.

Southwest Airlines provides a striking example of a successful company that puts attitude and interest at the top of its hiring agenda. Southwest is the most profitable company in its industry and enjoys a personnel turnover rate that is about half the industry average. Its hiring practices have a great deal to do with this. Southwest only hires people who are disposed to providing the friendly service that its customers expect and appreciate. With the exception of jobs that require technical skills, such as pilot, mechanic, and attorney, Southwest is less concerned with an applicant's toolkit of skills than with his or her attitude.

Southwest's approach to hiring is part of the corporate DNA created by its founder and retired CEO, Herb Kelleher. "If you don't have a good attitude," according to Kelleher, "we don't want you, no matter how skilled you are. We can change skill levels through training. We can't change attitude."[10] For Southwest, a good attitude means a sense of humor, a sense of teamwork, and a desire to make customers happy.

To determine a job candidate's core interests, try asking these questions during the interview:

- What have you most liked doing in your other jobs?

- What do you like to read? Or, if you're glancing at a newspaper or magazine, what kinds of articles and advertisements are most likely to catch your eye?

- What do you enjoy doing in your spare time?

- What stage of a project really excites you the most?

You can also show the candidate tables 2-1, 2-2, and 2-3 and ask him or her which one or more of the eight core business interests seem particularly appealing. Once you've determined where the job candidate's interests lie, you can determine whether those interests are a good fit for the open position.

Hiring for Microculture

Beyond matching the right person to the right job, finding the "right fit" has a cultural component. Jobs within organizations have cultural contexts, and you want to make sure that the person you're thinking of hiring will strengthen these contexts, not seriously conflict with them.

Consultant Dwight Gertz once described how a national chain of mall-based cookie shops inadvertently fell afoul of the "right fit" issue many years ago when its human resource department encouraged very self-directed people to apply for shop manager positions.

"We want independent people who want to be their own bosses," the recruiting literature stated. Once these people were hired and placed in the company's training program, however, they quickly discovered that everything from what to bake, when to bake it, and in which quantities was strictly determined by the company's operating manual. In reality, the company did not want entrepreneurs; it wanted people who could follow its time-tested procedures for running a mall cookie shop. It neither had nor encouraged an entrepreneurial culture. Not surprisingly, few of the new managers lasted more than a year.[11] There was a cultural mismatch between the company and the people it recruited.

Large and small companies alike have *macro-* and *microcultures,* and it's important that a job candidate can work effectively in each. A macroculture is an organization's way of doing things, its general values, the ways in which people relate to one another, and so forth. These same companies are likely to have *microcultures* as well—cultures that characterize different departments or job functions. For example, to the outside world, a particular organization may appear to have a very formal macroculture, with employees in serious-looking business suits and adhering to strict rules of conduct. Yet within this same organization there are likely to be many different microcultures: the software product-design department, for example, may be home to shaggy-haired engineers who dress in jeans and sneakers and who routinely play practical jokes on one another. The people and culture of the R&D department are probably very different from the "suits" who work in marketing and finance.

Your firm almost certainly has microcultures. Do you know what they are? The key to hiring right is to understand those microcultures and to choose people who will fit into, enjoy, and enrich them. So, if a job candidate truly enjoys wearing a formal suit to work every day and keeping conversations with colleagues strictly professional, she's probably not the right candidate for the funky, friendly little software group just down the hall!

If you find it difficult to define the culture of your unit or work group, the questionnaire in figure 2-1 can help you figure it out. Knowledge of the existing culture can help you hire new employees who will fit in and thrive.

FIGURE 2-1

Work Culture Survey

Our Current Work Atmosphere

How informed and involved do I/we feel in our group's overall strategy and decision making?

☐ Very ☐ Not at all

How do we dress for work?

☐ Formally ☐ Casually ☐ Mixed

How much spontaneous gathering for fun, breaks, and stress relief do we engage in?

☐ None ☐ Some ☐ A lot

How much do we get together outside of the office?

☐ None ☐ Some ☐ A lot

How much privacy and quiet do I/we have?

☐ None ☐ Some ☐ A lot

What kinds of *overall* culture do I/we think our group emphasizes? *Check as many as apply.*

☐ **Customer Service** (emphasizing creating internal and/or external customer solutions and getting close to customers by anticipating their needs and creating value for them)

☐ **Innovation** (emphasizing new ideas, processes and products, taking risks, embracing change, and so forth)

☐ **Operational Excellence** (emphasizing efficiency, effectiveness, *and* smooth operations)

☐ **Spirit** (emphasizing creating environments that inspire employee excellence and creativity, uplift people's spirits, unleash energy and enthusiasm, and strive toward a greater common goal)

Does our group's culture have enough "give" in it to accommodate different kinds of people, or is it a "love it or leave it" affair? (Be honest!)

More specifically, what parts of the culture does someone *have* to subscribe to in order to fit in?

Other important things about our culture (values, unspoken rules, etc.):

Ideas for Improving the Culture

Are there any important gaps between what kind of atmosphere you would like to work in and what kind of atmosphere currently characterizes our group? If so, what are they?

What measures might help improve our work culture and/or help close gaps between what we want or need and what exists?

Source: HMM Retaining Valued Employees.

Psychological Testing

MANAGER WANTED: A department of ISTPs (introverted sensing thinking perceivers) seeks an experienced ENTP (extraverted intuitive thinking perceiver) manager for a long-term and profitable relationship. No control-freaks or heavy judging types, please.

The use of psychological testing to screen job applicants is growing. In a 1998 American Management Association survey, 45 percent of 1,085 member companies reported administering one or more tests to job applicants, up from 35 percent in the previous year. Because of the time and expense involved, these tests are more often given to prospective managers than to lower-level employees, for whom tests of job skills are often more appropriate.[12]

Should you and your company use psychological testing? On the one hand, experts counsel caution. Unlike college-entrance exams, pre-employment tests aren't a rubber ruler for arbitrarily weeding out candidates. They can't provide a magic solution to your company's turnover problems. What's more, if you use the wrong test—or ask even a single inappropriate question—you expose your company to the threat of a lawsuit.

So why give these tests at all? One big reason: Used properly, psychological tests may predict success on the job better than any other measure. Among psychological tests, cognitive ability tests are the best. And personality tests, once generally viewed as worthless, have lately won some support from academic researchers. Testing has some built-in advantages over other means of selection, such as a lack of bias. A test asks the same questions and applies the same standards to everyone, and can thus counterbalance an interviewer's stereotypes. For example, a hiring executive may have a bias against people who are overweight or who didn't go to the "right" schools. A person's weight and school affiliation are not good predictors of success. But everyone involved in hiring decisions has biases—including some of which they may be unaware. Testing helps remove these biases. Psychological tests can also give a sense of how a prospective employee would fare within a company's culture.

Here are some tips from experts on how to make pre-employment testing work for your organization:

1. **Specify your hiring needs.** American Golf Corporation, headquartered in Santa Monica, California, has 1,000 managers overseeing more than 14,000 other employees in 270 locations across the country. American Golf has for years required all prospective managers to fill out a commercially available personality measure called the Predictive Index. "It has been useful," says Tom Norton, director of recruiting. "What we're careful of is matching [an applicant's] personality or work style to the supervisor they'd be working for. If someone really likes working with people and requires a lot of supervision, he or she probably wouldn't work well with an introvert."13

   American Golf's approach illustrates one of the main requirements (and advantages) of psychological tests: knowing what you're looking for. "It's important to look at what characteristics are being used in the job. That helps to guide what tests should be used," says William Harris, executive director of the Association of Test Publishers, a trade association based in Washington, D.C.14 Before administering tests, the hiring firm should understand the specific requirements of the job in question and the values and behaviors that define the workplace's culture. Indeed, some think that the self-study a company must undergo in preparation for using pre-employment tests is the most valuable component of the process.

2. **Don't rely on tests alone.** Think of testing as just one leg of a three-legged stool, with the candidate's record and conventional interviews being the other two. At American Golf, the personality measure "is one piece of many, many things we look at for each candidate," according to Norton. "It can validate other opinions we gather from things like interviews and references. It can sometimes raise an issue to look further into. [The test] is never anything we base a hiring decision on by itself."

3. **More is better (up to a point).** Tests aren't one-size-fits-all. To test for personality traits, experts advise instruments such as the Personality Research Form, WAIS-R, or the Executive Profile Survey. To examine a candidate's interests, try the Jackson Vocational Interest Survey. To measure cognitive ability (the term that has replaced IQ), a test such as the Watson-Glaser Critical Thinking Appraisal may be in order. It's not uncommon for companies and their consultants to give candidates several different tests at one sitting—one each for personality, interests, integrity, and cognitive ability, for example. A battery of tests in which each has some variance increases predictive power. Be warned, however, that the cost of testing will rise as more tests are administered. But given the costs involved in living with or firing a bad hiring choice, money spent on additional testing may be well spent—particularly when dealing with a top-management position.

4. **Psychological testing is not for amateurs.** Proper interpretation of results, even results of an off-the-shelf test, takes doctoral-level training in statistics, testing, and assessment. In fact, you cannot even get your hands on the test since distribution of the most powerful tests is strictly controlled to prevent misuse. Tests such as the Jackson Personality Inventory, the 16PF Personality Profile, and the Guilford-Zimmerman Temperament Survey are available only to members of organizations such as the American Psychological Association. Although there are no licensing requirements for test-givers and test consultants, the APA serves as a de facto licensing board, and psychologists found to have applied tests improperly can be decertified.

   The services of a consulting psychologist typically run about $1,500 to $2,000 per senior-level candidate, and the more extensive a screening, the higher the cost. A CEO screening may run somewhat higher.

5. **Beware of pitfalls.** Employment lawsuits are forcing testers to be very, very careful. Several laws and regulations of recent years—the Equal Employment Opportunity Commission's

rules, Congress's prohibition of lie detectors, and, most significantly, the American Disabilities Act of 1990 (ADA)—sharply restrict the content of pre-employment tests. One veteran of the testing business claims that his firm can now use only about 10 percent of the tests they once used; the remainder fall afoul of the rules. Retail chain Target Stores, for instance, goofed by giving job applicants its own test, which included questions from two standard tests that predated the ADA. The test included a few now-taboo questions on health, sexual preference, and religious beliefs. Target was sued in 1991 for employment discrimination and settled out of court for $2 million.

To be legally bulletproof, all questions on a pre-employment test must have predictive validity. That is, the test-giver must be able to show not only that a test accurately measures the traits it seeks to measure but also that it predicts behavior in the specific job in question. That's no small task, so test developers routinely spend millions of dollars and months or years on large-scale field studies before releasing a test. And every firm that uses them needs to validate the tests it uses with data from its own employees in order to be protected from litigation. It helps to have evidence that the tests work elsewhere, but the real key is to show that they work for you!

It is feasible for companies to construct their own tests, complete with predictive validity. For example, Procter & Gamble has designed a test that meets validation criteria for distinguishing the potential performance of a brand manager. Few companies, however, have the money and expertise to invest in the design of their own tests. Instead, they rely on testing consultants.

Summing Up

This chapter has elaborated on several specialized techniques that can improve your hiring process:

- Online recruiting is fast, inexpensive, and can increase your pool of candidates. Recruiting software can help you with this and make the material found on the Web more manageable.

- Professional recruiters can save you time. Although they come at a price, if you engage a competent one, your money will be well spent. Specialized firms have active networks of key people in the industries they serve and can get the word out quickly and confidentially to qualified people. They also screen respondents so that only qualified candidates are presented for evaluation.

- We considered the use of the "case interview" method—a useful way to measure a candidate's problem-solving ability. This method subjects a job applicant to a scenario and business problem similar to those encountered on the job. If you use this method, look for how candidates approach the problem, identify alternative solutions, and organize their thinking.

- Evaluating job applicants on the basis of embedded life interests is a macro approach to matching people up with jobs at which they will excel. Unless specific technical training is a prerequisite, many companies are better off hiring based on embedded interests than basing candidate choices on skills, which can often be easily taught.

- Hiring for cultural fit may be just as important as any other evaluation parameter. Culture defines an organization's ways of doing things, general values, and the ways in which people relate to one another. You want to avoid trying to fit a square peg into a round hole.

- Many companies are using psychological tests to learn more about people in the final candidates' pool. But exercise caution: Only deal with tests—and testing consultants—that can safely pass muster on the antidiscrimination front.

3

Keeping the Best

Essential Retention Strategies

Key Topics Covered in This Chapter

- *Why retention matters*

- *Why retention is now so challenging*

- *The special challenges of a diverse work force*

- *Why people stay—and why they leave*

- *Examples of companies that successfully retain employees*

- *Tips on managing for retention*

HIRING AND RETENTION are two sides of the same coin. They complement each other, and if both are done well they produce what every company desperately needs: first-class human assets. In this chapter we will shift our focus from the hiring process to strategies for keeping the good people you already have.

If you did everything described in the previous chapters right, and filled all your positions with only talented, hard-working people, you'd most likely have a considerable advantage over your competitors, since few companies ever accomplish this goal. But your hiring success would create another challenge: keeping those star employees on-board. After all, if your human assets were measurably superior, other companies would notice and try to lure them away with higher pay, more authority, and more appealing work situations—perhaps the same inducements you used to recruit them! You'd find yourself on the defensive, forced to look at your own employment practices, benefits, and compensation scheme to determine if these were unconsciously undermining bonds of loyalty between your company and the great people you've hired.

Retention is a challenge faced by many of the world's most admired companies. Consider the experience of many companies in the United States from 1992 to 2000. U.S. businesses enjoyed tremendous economic prosperity during this period and just about every able-bodied person who wanted a job was enlisted in the work force. In many employment categories—particularly high-skilled areas such as IT, software development, electrical engineering, accounting, and finance—demand outstripped supply, touching off what has become known as the "war for talent." Many companies recognized that a lack of human talent was a serious constraint on future growth and pulled all the stops in order to retain their most valuable employees. Ernst & Young went so far as to establish an Office of Retention with direct reporting responsibility to the CEO. Others set up work-life balance programs to alleviate stress on the home front. Casual dress regimens, on-site child care, and foosball tables proliferated. More than a few companies allowed employees to bring their dogs to work. Books and magazine articles on "how to keep your employees happy and productive" were cranked out by the score.

The great war for talent in the United States appeared to end with the recession that hit the country in late 2000. The high-tech sector was the first to be hit. Even IT professionals—the people formerly in greatest demand—were furloughed by the thousands. Layoffs followed in other industries as the recession rippled through the economy. Even Charles Schwab, a pioneer in the field of employee development and work-life balance, was forced to downsize. Between late 2000 and early 2002 the national unemployment rate almost doubled.

But recessions don't last forever, and most people recognized that the war for talent would heat up again once the economy got back on track. And in some sectors of the economy, the war never really subsided.

So, what is the retention situation in your business? Are all of your employees toiling happily in the company vineyards? Don't bet on it. According to a 1999 study of 2,000 employees by Hudson Institute and Walker Information:[1]

- 33 percent are "high risk"—that is, they are not committed to their present employer and not planning to stick around for the next two years;

- 39 percent are "trapped"—they aren't committed to the organization but are currently planning to stay for the next two years; and

- only 24 percent are "truly loyal"—both committed to the organization and planning to stay on for at least two years.

Thus, if your employees are anything like the ones surveyed, more than half are prepared (or preparing) to bolt!

This chapter is the first of several on the subject of employee retention. It explains why it is so important to your business—and so challenging. It offers insights into why people stay with their current employers and what factors influence them to leave. Two companies with remarkable success in employee retention are highlighted as examples: Southwest Airlines and SAS Institute. Finally, this chapter offers suggestions on what you can do to retain your best people.

Why Retention Matters

Retention is the converse of turnover (turnover being the sum of voluntary and involuntary separations between an employee and his or her company). Industry-wide and company-specific measures that track turnover rates reveal that most companies surveyed by the Center for Organizational Research had turnover rates in the 15 to 50 percent range, though a sizable minority enjoyed single-digit turnover (see figure 3-1).

Retention isn't simply a "feel good" issue. The retention of good employees matters for three important bottom-line reasons: 1) the growing importance of intellectual capital; 2) a causal link between employee tenure and customer satisfaction; and 3) the high cost of employee turnover. Let's examine each of these in turn.

The Importance of Intellectual Capital

During the Industrial Age, a firm's physical assets—such as machinery, plants, and even land—determined how strongly it could compete. In the current "Knowledge Era," intellectual capital is what defines a company's competitive edge. Intellectual capital is the unique knowledge and skills that a company's work force possesses. Today's successful businesses win with innovative new ideas and

FIGURE 3-1

How Bad Is Turnover?

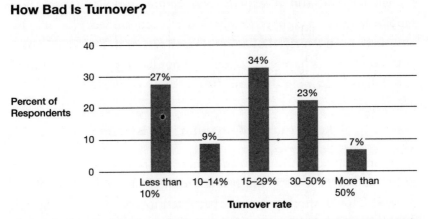

Most companies surveyed by the Center for Organizational Research had annual turnover rates in the 15%–50% range, though a sizable minority continues to enjoy rates below 10%. The average rate: 23%.

Source: Center for Organizational Research, a division of Linkage Inc., 2001.

top-notch products and services—all of which originate in the knowledge and skills of employees. Examples of people who possess intellectual capital include computer programmers, network engineers, technical designers, CPAs, and direct-marketing analysts. Other possessors of intellectual capital are:

- mid-level managers (they know whom to contact to get things done)

- top-level executives (they have years of business savvy and industry knowledge)

- strategic-planning/business-development professionals (they know how to do competitive and other forms of analysis)

- human resource professionals (they understand recruiting, employment law, compensation, and other critical employee-relations issues)

- in-house legal counsel (they understand intellectual property, securities, and other areas of business law)

Whenever employees leave, the company loses their hard-won knowledge and (often expensively) acquired skills. When those employees go to a competitor, the loss is compounded. Not only has your firm been deprived of an important part of its knowledge base, your competitors have gained it—without having to invest the time and dollars in training that your firm may have invested.

Retention and Customer Satisfaction

Everyone understands that customer satisfaction is one of the most—if not *the* most—important factors in business survival and growth. This is another reason that retention is so critical. Simply stated: *Employees who are satisfied with their work and their company are more likely to create satisfied customers.* Although this may be intuitively obvious, a growing body of research supports this correlation.

This fact was amply illustrated by Sears Roebuck, which in the early 1990s was rapidly losing money and customers. A new management team led by Arthur Martinez was brought in to stop the losses and revitalize the aging retail giant. As reported in a landmark *Harvard Business Review* article, one of the initiatives undertaken by the new management team was a study that involved eight hundred company stores and thousands of store personnel.[2] That study examined a number of important relationships and found that:

- negative employee attitudes and behaviors adversely affected the satisfaction of Sears customers;

- high employee turnover reduced customer satisfaction and store revenues; and

- the extent to which store employees understood their jobs and the company's strategic objectives had a direct bearing on their attitudes and behaviors.

The study concluded that employees' attitudes toward their work and toward Sears were both poor and that these attitudes were producing employee behaviors that measurably reduced customer satisfaction and sales revenues. Using these insights, the Sears team developed an "employee-customer profit chain model" that quantified the causal links between employees' attitudes, job tenure, and the financial performance of the store in which they worked. They even formulated metrics capable of *predicting* the impact of employee attitude, tenure, and behaviors on revenues. (See "Case Study: Retention and the Service-Profit Chain" for some history behind the creation of this model.)

Sears's findings are echoed by many other studies, including a multicompany project that concluded that "employee attachment predicts customer attachment. When employees feel an attachment to the firm, they are more likely to share their positive images and feelings about the firm with customers. When customers are exposed to favorable testimonials, they respond more favorably to the firm."[3] Likewise, a William M. Mercer survey of senior human resource executives in large enterprises reported that "more than half of (study) participants see poor customer service as a consequence of attraction and retention problems."[4]

The Cost of Turnover

The high price of turnover is the third major reason that retention matters. Employee turnover involves three types of costs, each of which saps bottom-line results:

- Direct expenses, including the out-of-pocket cost of recruiting, interviewing, and training replacements. (In a tight labor market, replacements may require a higher salary than the people who are defecting—not to mention the potential cost of signing bonuses.)

- Indirect costs, such as the effect on workload, morale, and customer satisfaction. Will other employees consider quitting? Will customers follow the employee who left?

- Opportunity costs, including lost knowledge and the work that doesn't get done while managers and other employees focus on filling the slot and bringing the replacement up to speed.

Case Study: Retention and the Service-Profit Chain

The Sears employee-customer profit chain model is a methodological descendent of an earlier model developed by Harvard Business School professors James Heskett, Earl Sasser, and several associates. Called the "service-profit chain," it likewise recognizes the role of employee satisfaction, loyalty, and retention.

Seven fundamental propositions form the links of the service-profit chain:

1. Customer loyalty drives profitability and growth. A 5 percent increase in customer loyalty can boost profits by 25 to 85 percent.

2. Customer satisfaction drives customer loyalty. Xerox found that "very satisfied" customers were six times more likely to repurchase company equipment than were customers who were merely "satisfied."

3. Value drives customer satisfaction. An insurer's efforts to deliver maximum value include funding a team that provides special services at the sites of major catastrophes. The company has one of the highest margins in its industry.

4. Employee productivity drives value. Southwest Airlines deplanes and reloads two-thirds of its flights in fifteen minutes or less; pilots fly an average of twenty hours more per month than their competitors. Fares stay low while service remains high.

5. Employee loyalty drives productivity. One auto dealer's annual cost of replacing a sales rep who had eight years of experience with one who had less than a year was $432,000 in lost sales.

6. Employee satisfaction drives loyalty. In one company study, 30 percent of all dissatisfied employees expressed an intention to leave, compared to only 10 percent of all satisfied employees. Moreover, low employee turnover was found to be closely linked to high customer satisfaction.

7. Internal quality drives employee satisfaction. Service workers are happiest when they are empowered to make things right for customers and when they have responsibilities that add depth to their work.

SOURCE: James Heskett, Thomas Jones, Gary Loveland, W. Earl Sasser, Jr., and Leonard Schlesinger, "Putting the Service-Profit Chain to Work," *Harvard Business Review* 72, no. 2 (March–April 1994): 164–172.

What do these add up to? Estimates vary widely, in part because the cost of losing and replacing an employee depends on the individual and the industry involved. But it is rarely low. For employees in general, the U.S. Department of Labor estimates a turnover cost of about one-third the new person's salary. Among managerial and professional employees, the percentage increases dramatically. Generally, estimates are in the range of one to two times the departee's annual salary. Those figures mask lots of variability, however, much of it related to the effectiveness of the departing employee. The cost of losing a highly effective employee is obviously much higher than the cost of losing an average performer—even though the salaries and benefits of the two may be very similar. To help estimate your cost of employee turnover, please visit www.elearning.hbsp.org/businesstools to access an employee turnover calculator.

Employment categories such as information technology, software programming, management consulting, and public auditing routinely experience turnover rates of 20 to 25 percent. Considering salary levels in these fields, those rates must result in a painful financial burden for the affected company.

There is another side to the cost-of-turnover coin. The turnover of incompetent people may not produce any cost since the departure of such employees may actually eliminate certain hidden costs. Consider, for example, the costs of having mediocre or incompetent people in key positions, as cited in the introduction to this book. What is the cost of the poor decisions often made by such employees? Bradford Smart has estimated the cost of an inept middle manager at roughly $1.2 million per year. The price tag goes up as you consider incompetence at the senior management level. And what is the cost associated with the poor morale and defections they create? That's anyone's guess.

Why Retention Is So Challenging

The challenge of retaining good employees is complicated by a number of factors: demographic conditions, cultural expectations, and upheavals in the world of work.

Demographics

In some countries, most notably the United States, demographic changes have made retention especially challenging. Here are just a few of the remarkable statistics from the American scene:

- The work force overall is maturing. Currently, the average age of employees is 35. Some 3.75 million workers have already turned 55. By 2015, the population of Americans in the prime management age range of 35–45 will be 15 percent less than it was in 2000. (See figure 3-2.)

- Economic growth is outpacing the growth of the work force. The U.S. economy has been growing at 2.4 percent while growth in the labor force lags behind at only 1.2 percent.

- The supply of highly skilled technicians and professionals is being overwhelmed by demand—particularly in computer-related fields.

The ramifications of these trends are clear: a pronounced shortage of skilled workers—and escalating competition among companies to recruit and retain those that are available.

FIGURE 3-2

The Aging Work Force

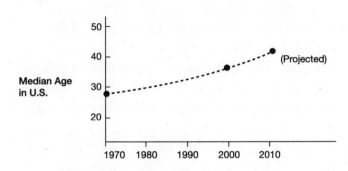

Source: HMM Retaining Valued Employees.

Cultural Expectations

People's expectations about work also strongly influence retention patterns. In some countries, for example, employees often spend their entire lifetime working for one firm. Employees, their colleagues, and companies consider one another almost as family, and give each other the same dedication, commitment, and support that one would give family members. In contrast, the cultures of other countries emphasize fast-moving and continual change—including rapid "job-hopping" by workers in search of the best possible combination of work, compensation, and future opportunities. Some countries' employment laws—particularly in France, Germany, and Italy—make it difficult to fire or lay off workers, while in other regions companies can freely let employees go.

As you might guess, a company's retention goals might be more or less challenging depending on the cultural factors that shape its region's or industry's employment trends.

Upheavals in the World of Work

Finally, changing economic and cultural circumstances can produce dramatic upheavals in the work world. Here are just a few examples:

- A trend toward free agency. Free agents—self-employed workers who serve various clients on a temporary, contract basis—
  now make up 15 percent of the American work force.

- The dissolving employer/employee contract. With the wave of
  reengineering and restructuring that hit many parts of the
  business world in the 1970s and 1980s—and again in the
  2000–2002 business downturn—some companies downplayed
  the importance of the work force. As a result, old assumptions
  about employer paternalism and employee loyalty evaporated.
  Today, most workers assume that they must take charge of their
  own employability and careers—even if that means moving
  from firm to firm. In the United States alone, most people will
  hold 8.6 different jobs between the ages of 18 and 32.

- An intensifying need for technical skills. Economic development around the globe, the emergence of the Internet economy, and accelerating advances in technology in general have
  increased the demand for people with advanced technical skills.
  With a global marketplace for technical labor, competition will
  be intense and come from unlikely quarters.

- A growth in Internet recruiting. As described in the previous
  chapter, the Internet has made it easier for employees to learn
  about—and apply for—jobs at other companies. And it's no
  longer just the young folks who are computer savvy enough to
  surf the Web for the perfect job. Workers of all ages and backgrounds are feeling more and more comfortable using the
  Internet to explore outside job opportunities.

- Demands for greater work-life balance. In the United States,
  where two-earner households are commonplace, many are
  simply fed up with workplace hours and practices that put
  corporate needs ahead of personal and family obligations.
  Weekend meetings. Vacations interrupted by e-mails from the
  office. Too many hotel nights. Long daily commutes. Many
  employees, particularly women with young children, are walk-
  ing away to take lower-paying jobs nearer to home or finding
  other situations that make work-life balance more feasible.

When you put these trends together, it's clear that companies can no longer expect employees to join them early in life and stay indefinitely. Instead, firms must actively and creatively encourage good people to stay—especially in high-tech markets.

The Special Challenges of a Diverse Work Force

Retention is especially challenging when the work force is highly diverse. And this is the type of work force that managers in many parts of the world today face. From age and gender, to part-time versus full-time status, to ethnicity, race, sexual orientation, and physical ability—companies are both benefiting from and struggling with differences among employees. "One-size-fits-all" strategies for keeping good people simply don't work any longer. Companies can best improve their retention rates by crafting creative, specialized strategies for each major segment of the work force.

The Contingent Work Force

Members of the "contingent work force"—part-timers, contractors, and temporary employees—offer some important advantages, as well as difficult challenges, for managers and HR departments. Primary advantages include:

- Flexibility—companies can customize these workers' schedules to meet current work flow and demands, using them only when needed.

- Affordability—firms save money on payroll taxes, health benefits, and other expenses by employing temps, part-timers, or freelancers.

Challenges include:

- High turnover—sometimes as much as 200 to 300 percent—which introduces unpredictability and instability into the firm's culture.

- A lower degree of loyalty to the firm and its products.

- A growing demand for the same benefits that regular employees receive—such as satisfying work and career-development
  support.

Because the contingent work force is such a valuable resource, many
companies are now developing programs designed specifically to
retain these employees. For example, one company offers contingent
work force members skills training in exchange for a six-month
commitment.

Younger Workers

Younger workers—primarily those in their twenties—bring energy,
freshness, and state-of-the-art technical knowledge into a firm's
work force. Demographic trends, in the United States especially,
have created an unprecedented shortage of these workers, who
are often referred to as "Gen-Xers." These workers pose some
difficulties:

- Young workers are particularly interested in defining their
  career paths and taking jobs that will help them advance to
  their *next* jobs.

- Many young workers are more comfortable with rapid change
  and flat management structures than are older employees. This
  can create misunderstandings and tensions between the two
  generations at work—especially when a supervisor and a direct
  report hail from different generations and have different work
  expectations.

- Many young employees want their employer to define a career
  ladder for them—a professional track that will let them build
  up to a level of compensation that will enable them to support
  young families.

How can your firm meet its younger workers' needs and thus retain
the best among them? These four strategies can help:

1. **Understand their background, and customize their work accordingly.** These young people know about "downsizing" from the experience of their parents; they have accepted the truth that nothing is certain in the corporate world. Consequently, they're most loyal to their own skills. If there is any group for which job modification or a "stretch" assignment is not only a good but an *essential* idea, it's this one. At the same time, they're comfortable with timesaving and instant-communication devices (e-mail, instant messaging, and the Internet) and so tend to perform tasks quickly. Thus short-deadline, multifaceted projects may be especially appealing to them.

2. **Include professional development in your value proposition to this group.** To appeal to younger workers, your firm can demonstrate its commitment to supporting and clarifying their career paths (for example, through high-tech career-management resources like the Internet and job boards).

3. **Lead through learning.** Employees in their twenties place a high priority on learning and developing new skills. Provide teaching and coaching on a regular basis, as well as mentoring and internship programs. Give new recruits the opportunity to learn about the rest of the company by allowing employees to make presentations about their departments and jobs.

4. **Seek independent, continuous feedback from all employees.** Capitalize on this group's everyday learning by soliciting continuous feedback through any of the new online tools available today.

50+ Employees

Employees in this age group merit special attention for two reasons. First, for some companies they represent a sizeable percentage of their employees. Second, mature workers (in the United States, the "baby boomer" generation) have extensive knowledge and rich business experience—they thus embody a major portion of any firm's intellectual capital. Many have life skills such as reliability, patience, or fair-mindedness—the types of hard-won skills that people gain only by grappling with day-to-day responsibilities over many years. According to the author of the article "How to Keep Your 50-Somethings," these employees also pose several difficulties for companies:[5]

- They are moving closer and closer to retirement each day. As they begin to retire, whole plants or departments may be decimated.

- In regions where the economy is booming, many older workers are setting their sights on early retirement, a second career, or a better job somewhere else.

- Others may become sick or injured or will leave to care for an aging parent—and never return.

To keep boomers on your payroll *and* productive, you may have to create a workplace in which conventional wisdom about job descriptions, hours, pay, benefits, and so on go out the window. Keep these four tips in mind:

- **Ask mature workers what they need.** Merely opening a dialogue in this way can help you better serve this age group's needs. For example, many older workers may value long-term health care insurance more than a big raise.

- **Support flexibility.** Life seems shorter at 50-plus; many employees at this age want to work part-time, job-share, or telecommute. They're also interested in sabbaticals, unpaid time off, and released time for community projects. Consider any of these offerings, as well as "phased retirement," which lets employees reduce their hours in stages rather than all at once.

- **Make their work interesting.** On the job, many boomers want autonomy, a sense of meaning, and a chance to keep learning. This can mean redesigning the way tasks get done. Let mature employees work on their own, and provide whatever training they need to pick up new skills—particularly in the area of technology.

- **Tailor your compensation system.** Avoid "one-size-fits-all" pay
  plans. For example, while younger employees may want cash,
  older ones may prefer larger contributions to a retirement fund.
  Be creative!

Female Employees

In the United States and many other Westernized societies, the end
of World War II triggered an unprecedented flood of women into
the workplace. Now, that trend is reversing—in some alarming ways.
For instance, women are leaving corporate America at *twice* the rate
of men—many of them trading the corporate world for the entrepreneurial frontier. Why? Many corporate women are discouraged
by the "glass ceiling" that blocks their advancement. Others want or
need more flexibility than their employers can provide. Still others—like their male counterparts—have developed business concepts that they would rather pursue as individuals than as employees
of some faceless corporation. The resulting "brain drain" carries a
heavy price.

How can your firm respond? Try these four strategies:[6]

1. **Analyze the current situation.** Identify how many women hold
   upper-management positions in your firm and how many are
   in the pipeline. Then talk with these women—find out what's
   important to them, and then find ways to meet their needs.

2. **Eradicate "invisible" barriers to women's success.** Take a hard
   look at your corporate environment. Barriers to female success
   can be subtle—but very real. Identify high-potential women
   and give them equal access to career-enhancing opportunities:
   line positions, skill-building opportunities, special project
   assignments, committee leadership, and appointment to high-
   visibility teams.

3. **Cultivate support throughout the organization.** For example,
   hold supervisors responsible for meeting the company's gender-
   equity goals. Assign an ombudsman to handle any bias inci-
   dents. Send a message from the top that signals acceptance of a

broad range of leadership styles and an invitation to top talent—male *and* female—to progress through the ranks.

4. **Promote the understanding that women's ways of managing are
good for business.** Many older books on management advise
women to act like men in order to succeed. Today, a wealth of
research contradicts this approach. Specifically, numerous female
entrepreneurs offer more flexibility, understanding, and an open
management style—all of which can give their corporations a
vital competitive edge.

There are many ways to address gender concerns in the workplace.
No matter how you choose to do so, communication, creativity, and
a proactive approach will help.

Race, Ethnicity, Sexual Orientation, and Other Differences

Human beings have a long history of treating one another unfairly
because of differences—whether the difference is race, ethnicity,
sexual orientation, physical ability, or another characteristic. Many
people have suffered discrimination in the workplace—sometimes
covert, sometimes open—if they didn't fit in with what others
thought of as the "mainstream" culture. This kind of unfair treatment
carries a high price for businesses.

Companies can't afford to neglect the talent found among people who are "different." Every talented employee counts, and finding
ways to keep them simply makes good business sense. So, how can
your firm benefit from—and sustain—the many forms of diversity
represented in its work force? Observe the four points identified
above with respect to women. Remember, too, that members of
nonmainstream groups are keenly alert to insincere gestures aimed at
mollifying them. They'll be watching to see if your organization will
"walk the talk." Promises made but not delivered will not go unno-
ticed. At the same time, promoting unqualified nonmainstream
employees will alienate *everyone*. Also, if the opportunities for growth
and advancement aren't really there, pretending and proclaiming that
they are will only hurt your organization.

Why People Stay

People stay with a company for many different reasons, including job security, a work culture that recognizes the importance of work-life balance, recognition for a job well done, flexible hours, or a sense of belonging. These reasons can vary widely from country to country. However, in cultures in which it's assumed that people may freely change jobs, the major motivations for staying are:

- **Pride in the organization.** People want to work for well-managed companies headed by skilled, resourceful leaders—that is, top-level managers who have a clear vision of the firm's future, who can devise powerful strategies for success, and who can motivate others to realize that vision.

- **A respected supervisor.** Even more important is the employee-supervisor relationship. People are more likely to stay if they have a supervisor whom they respect and who is supportive of them.

- **Fair compensation.** People also want to work for companies that offer fair compensation. This includes not only competitive wages and benefits but also intangible compensation in the form of opportunities to learn, grow, and achieve.

- **Affiliation.** The chance to work with respected and compatible colleagues is another element that many people consider essential.

- **Meaningful work.** Finally, people want to work for companies that let them do the kinds of work that appeal to their deepest interests. Satisfying and stimulating work makes all of us more productive.

The findings of the McKinsey & Company "War for Talent 2000 Survey" of middle and senior managers generally supported these findings. That survey asked managers how important various factors are in their decisions to join and stay with a company. The results are shown in figure 3-3. The bold items are those that have a

FIGURE 3-3

What Managers Are Looking For

% of respondents who rate the item critical in their decision of which company to join and stay with

Exciting work

✓ **Interesting, challenging work**	**59%**
✓ **Work I feel passionate about**	**45%**
I am listened to and can impact decisions	41%
Take initiative and own success	40%
Have impact in the company	35%
Freedom and autonomy	31%
Participate in strategic directions	22%
Encouraged to innovate	22%

Development

✓ **Career advancement opportunities**	**37%**
✓ **Long-term commitment to me**	**35%**
✓ **Build skills to boost career**	**35%**
✓ **Sr. managers committed to me**	**30%**
✓ **High performers promoted**	**28%**
Frequent feedback	17%
Receive helpful mentoring	16%
Ongoing training	14%

Lifestyle

Can meet my personal/family commitments	51%
Live in appealing city/region	34%
Reasonable work pace	11%
Flexibility of when/where I work	9%

Great company

✓ **Company is well managed**	**48%**
✓ **Good relations with my boss**	**43%**
✓ **I like the culture and values**	**39%**
✓ **I trust senior management**	**38%**
Not hampered by bureaucracy	30%
✓ **A boss I admire**	**26%**
Exciting, interesting industry	24%
Industry has growth prospects	22%
Products make a difference	21%
Company is a strong performer	21%
People are high performers	19%
Company's reputation	17%
Camaraderie with colleagues	13%
Contribution beyond the bottom line	9%
People with diverse backgrounds	8%
Positive impact on society	6%

Wealth and rewards

✓ **Recognized, rewarded for my individual contribution**	**39%**
✓ **Substantial wealth creation opportunity**	**36%**
✓ **High performers paid more**	**31%**
✓ **Annual cash comp is high**	**26%**

✓ **Bolded** = items that make up the elements that have a strong causal relationship with satisfaction

Source: McKinsey & Company War for Talent 2000 Survey, reprinted with permission.

strong causal relationship with the overall level of reported satisfaction. Authors Ed Michaels, Helen Handfield-Jones, and Beth Axelrod make a case from these and other findings that companies can attract and retain talented people if they pay attention to what they term the "employee value proposition," or EVP. EVP is the workplace equivalent to the value proposition that every company knowingly or unknowingly offers its customers: a measure of perceived value for a particular cost. They suggest that if companies want to be more successful at attracting and retaining talent, they should evaluate and strengthen their value propositions to employees:

> *To create a compelling employee value proposition, a company must provide the core elements that managers look for—exciting work, a great company, attractive compensation, and opportunities to develop. A few more perks, casual dress, or more generous health plans won't make the difference between a weak EVP and a strong one. If you want to substantially strengthen your company's EVP, be prepared to change things as fundamental as the business strategy, the organization structure, the culture, and even the caliber of leaders.*[7]

Though the data on which Michaels et al. base their conclusions focused on managers and executives, it's likely that other employees will respond similarly.

Why People Leave

People also leave organizations for many different reasons, but primarily because one or more of the above conditions was either absent at the beginning or has since been eliminated. For example:

- **The company's leadership shifts.** Either the quality of top management's decisions declines, or new leaders—whom employees don't yet trust or feel comfortable with—take the helm.

- **Conflict with immediate supervisors.** People may also leave when their relationship with their bosses becomes stressful or problematic, and they don't see any other options in their company. (See "Managers and Supervisors Are Key" for more on this topic.)

- **Close friends leave.** One or more colleagues whom an employee particularly likes and respects leave the firm, thus taking away an affiliation that is very meaningful to that employee.

Managers and Supervisors Are Key

You can have terrific pay and benefits, employee-friendly policies, and all the other things that induce loyalty and retention, but a few rotten apples can spoil the barrel. Specifically, a bad manager can neutralize every retention scheme you put in place. Gallup researchers Marcus Buckingham and Curt Coffman put it this way:

> *Managers trump companies. It's not that . . . employee-focused initiatives are unimportant. It's just that your immediate manager is more important. She defines and pervades your work environment. . . . [I]f your relationship with your manager is fractured, then no amount of in-chair massaging or company-sponsored dog walking will persuade you to stay and perform. It is better to work for a great manager in an old-fashioned company than for a terrible manager in a company offering an enlightened, company-focused culture.* [a]

Beth Axelrod, Helen Handfield-Jones, and Ed Michaels of McKinsey & Company reached a similar conclusion about bad managers, which they describe as "C performers." "[K]eeping C performers in leadership positions lowers the bar for everyone—a clear danger for any company that wants to create a performance-focused culture. C performers hire other C performers, and their continued presence discourages the people around them, makes the company a less attractive place for highly talented people, and calls in question the judgment of senior leaders." [b] (We have more on C performers and how to handle them in a later chapter.)

While many say that the company culture is what matters in retention, the culture of operating units is what really matters to the people who work in them. If the boss is a jerk or an incompetent, the best people will leave.

[a] Marcus Buckingham and Curt Coffman, *First, Break at the Rules* (New York: Simon & Schuster, 1999), 34.
[b] Beth Axelrod, Helen Handfield-Jones, and Ed Michaels, "A New Game for C Players," *Harvard Business Review* 80, no. 1 (January 2002): 83.

- **An unfavorable change of responsibilities.** A person's job
  responsibilities change so that the work no longer appeals to his
  or her deepest interests or provides meaning or stimulation.

Perhaps the number-one point to keep in mind when thinking
about why people leave is this: People most often leave for the
wrong reasons. That is, they leave without really understanding *why*
they're unhappy or *what* opportunities to improve things may exist
within the company. Thus they jump from company to company,
making the same mistake each time. Consider this example:

> *An engineer is promoted to a managerial position because he's a high
> performer and has been with the company for a while. This person may
> not even like being a manager. But because he hasn't yet identified his
> deepest work interests, he doesn't make the connection between his new
> role and his unhappiness. Instead, he concludes that he just doesn't like
> the company anymore—and starts looking for another job.*
>
> *Unfortunately, when he finds another job outside the company, it'll
> likely be another managerial position. He'll work at that job for a
> while before realizing that he's still unhappy—at which point he will
> decide that the new company, too, is a bad fit for him.*

Mid-level managers seem to repeat this pattern more than any
other employee group.

Two Retention Champions

Most people recognize Southwest Airlines as a highly successful
company. In an industry plagued by strikes, desperate mergers, and
buckets of red ink, Texas-based SWA boasts thirty consecutive profitable years—something that no other major airline can do. Less
well-known is the fact that SWA's employee turnover rate is just
over 4 percent, half that of its competitors. People who sign on as
SWA employees clearly like their jobs and stick around, cutting the
company's recruiting and training costs. And high employee morale
rubs off on customers, making them satisfied and loyal users.

SWA's strong relationship with its employees is the legacy of
Herb Kelleher, who created an employee-focused workplace based

on informality, camaraderie, teamwork, and dedication to customer satisfaction. Just as he differentiated his product with his business strategy (low price, no frills, on-time), he differentiated SWA's value proposition to its employees. Studies of the SWA work environment indicate that it delivers on the qualities we've already identified under "why people stay"—pride in the organization, compatible supervisors, fair compensation, affiliation, and meaningful work.

Also with a turnover rate of just over 4 percent, SAS Institute is another retention champion. Its low employee turnover is even more remarkable given that SAS is in the software development business, where turnover generally runs in the 20 to 25 percent range. Most of its 8,000-plus employees could walk away from their jobs and quickly land new ones—and probably at higher pay rates. But they don't.

SAS's secret for employee retention is a working environment that few would ever trade. *Fast Company* magazine did a feature story on SAS several years ago, describing it as "Sanity, Inc.," a calm and humane place in a high-pressure world.[8] The SAS work environment has many features that employees appear to value highly: individual offices for all, flexible work schedules and programs that help employees integrate their work and family responsibilities, an on-site health facility, and unlimited sick days. Parents can use the company's on-site day care facility and even have lunch with their children. Most unusual of all is the fact that the company's Cary, North Carolina, campus headquarters closes at 6 P.M.

It would be easy to dismiss the SAS approach as too soft-hearted and soft-headed to be sustainable in the hardball software industry. But the company has a long-term record of growth and profitability. Its high spending on employee-friendly programs doesn't come out of potential profits but from the millions it would otherwise spend on employee turnover. The company has calculated what it saves through its low turnover rate (relative to its competitors) and used those savings to fund a better life- and work-style for everyone on the payroll. Figuring that it saves somewhere between $50 million and $70 million per year in turnover costs, SAS estimates that it can spend six to eight thousand dollars per employee on workplace enhancement. And it is still ahead of the game when you figure the greater productivity of teams that stay together, the knowledge that stays in the company, and the bonds that link customers to individual employees.

Managing for Retention: An Overview

So what can managers do to keep as many good employees as possible? Here's a short list that will cover most of the bases. We'll get into more details on many of these points later in this book.

1. **Get people off to a good start.** Getting people off to a good start begins with hiring people who are suited to their jobs and making sure that they understand what they are getting into (both in terms of the culture of the company and the specifics of their job descriptions). A good start also begins with a new-employee orientation that makes them feel welcomed and part of the group.

2. **Create a great environment—with bosses whom people respect.** Managers often assume that company policies and corporate culture determine the working environment. They do, to an extent. But policies can be circumvented. In any case, the atmosphere in a department or unit is more important to individual employees than the culture of the corporation as a whole. How does your unit stack up on this score?

   Bad bosses are not conducive to a great environment. How many of your unit's managers or supervisors are repellent to their reports? How many have temper tantrums, berate their charges in public, blame others for their own failures, or never have the sense to say "Thanks, you're doing a good job"? If your managers or supervisors are repellent, count on every employee with marketable skills to leave.

   In the end, it's better to replace bad managers and supervisors than to replace an endless stream of employees.

3. **Share information.** Freely dispensing information—about the business, about financial performance, about strategies and plans—tells employees that you trust them, that they are important partners, and that you respect their ability to understand and contribute to the business as a whole.

4. **Give people as much autonomy as they can handle.** Many people enjoy working with a minimum of supervision. So, give people as long a leash as they can handle. Doing so will make them happy and make your job as manager easier. Send a team off on its own with the charge of exploring a new market or solving a business problem. If it's feasible, carve out a whole business unit and let its members work on their own.

5. **Challenge people to stretch.** Most people—particularly the ones you want most to retain—enjoy a challenge and the feeling that you've entrusted them with bigger responsibilities than they had a right to expect. So put the people you want most to retain into jobs that will make them stretch—and give them the support they need to succeed.

6. **Be flexible.** A survey by Ceridian Employer Services (in Minneapolis) confirmed what savvy managers already know: Flexible work arrangements are highly successful in retaining employees. Nearly two-thirds of Ceridian's respondents felt that virtual teams, flexible work plans, and telecommuting were effective in boosting retention. To be sure, not every manager has the authority to create whole new work arrangements. But nearly everybody can allow some on-the-spot flexibility, letting employees rearrange work to care for a sick child, for example, or to keep a doctor's appointment. Today's harried employees value that kind of flexibility highly.

7. **Design jobs to encourage retention.** Nothing is more soul-deadening for an intelligent contributor than a job that is too repetitive, too isolated, insufficiently challenging, or downright unpleasant. So if you see unacceptable high turnover in a critical job category, take a good look at what you're asking

people in that job to do every day. You may be able to cure the turnover problem through job redesign: adding variety to a repetitive job, engaging isolated employees in occasional team projects, upping the challenge, and so forth. If a job involves one or more repugnant tasks, consider eliminating or outsourcing those tasks.

8. **Identify potential defectors early.** Great work environments and great jobs are a matter of opinion; what challenges one person may terrify another. You won't know how well you're doing on either score unless you ask.

   As a manager, you routinely interact and share views with your direct reports. Think about adding "defection detection" to these communications. Doing so will help you identify potential defectors in time to take effective countermeasures. Conduct a "stay interview" by asking people how they feel about their assignments, company policies, and the working environment. Ask about individual goals, whether they feel included or excluded by the corporate culture, and what would keep them with the company. For an interactive tool on conducting a stay interview, please visit *www.elearning.hbsp.org/businesstools*. Hartford Life starts this process six months after an employee is hired, with a formal session asking what employees think about the company. (See "Tips for Detecting Potential Defectors" for more information about this process.)

   While you're at it, get feedback on your performance as a manager. Arrow Electronics uses a "360-degree feedback" system, monitored by the CEO to determine whether its managers are actually providing the feedback and coaching that they should.

9. **Be a retention-oriented manager.** Never forget that part of your responsibility as a manager is to assure proper staffing in your unit. Retaining good and excellent performers is part that job. So look at how you manage people and how you schedule work flow. Are you the kind of boss who manages in ways that encourage the best people to stay, or are you unknowingly driving them away?

Tips for Detecting Potential Defectors

Are some of your people considering leaving? B. Lynn Ware, founder of the retention consulting firm ITS, Inc., counsels clients to watch for early signs of dissatisfaction and disaffection, including:

- a change in behavior, such as coming in later or leaving earlier;

- a decline in performance;

- sudden complaints from a person who hasn't been a complainer;

- wistful references to other companies (for example, "I heard of this guy who got a $30,000 signing bonus at XYZ Company");

- withdrawal behavior (for example, an employee who had always participated in meetings or volunteered for projects, suddenly stays in the background or does just enough to get by); and

- talk about "burnout."

If you see one of these warning signals, get right on it. Arrange to meet with the employee as soon as possible. Use probing questions to identify the source of the problem. Indicate that you value him or her as an employee, and ask how you can work together to creating a better work experience.

SOURCE: "Employee Retention: What Managers Can Do," *Harvard Management Update,* April 2000.

Summing Up

This chapter has described major issues relating to employee retention and highlighted ways in which managers can make a difference. In particular:

- Retention matters because high turnover creates high replacement costs and is clearly associated with low levels of customer satisfaction, customer loyalty, and lost revenues.

- Retention is particularly challenging today due to a number of factors—in particular, an aging work force and a growing imbalance in the supply and demand of qualified personnel. In addition, today's workers have different expectations about work-life balance.

- People stay with their employers when they see the organization as a source of pride and affiliation, when they respect their supervisors, when they are fairly compensated, and when they perceive their work as meaningful.

- People seek greener pastures when leadership changes unfavorably, when they are in conflict with their immediate superiors, when close friends depart, and when their responsibilities change in ways that they do not favor.

- Managers can make a difference by following the nine "Managing for Retention" points outlined in this chapter.

Market–Wise Retention

Competing in the War for Talent

Key Topics Covered in This Chapter

- *Differentiating between employees in terms of economic value to the organization*

- *Seven market-based strategies for improving retention*

EVERY LARGE ORGANIZATION has a distribution of low, average, and high performers. Nevertheless, most corporate retention programs—which are typically expensive to implement—don't differentiate between them. At the same time, every organization is subject to labor market forces over which it has little or no control. There is likely to be a "buyer's market" for some job categories and a "seller's market" for others. Thus, a company must do its best to identify which employees—or employee segments—represent the highest value to the organization, and then apply its resources in a manner that optimizes their retention in a free labor marketplace.[1]

Not All Employees Have Equal Value

The human resources people who toil in the field of hiring and retention are no strangers to the labor market which, like every market, is subject to the laws of supply and demand. They also understand the cost of replacing personnel. Those experiences do not, however, always find their way into retention efforts and programs. In this regard they would benefit from the experience of their colleagues in the marketing department.[2]

Marketing people know that some customers—generally identified as customer segments—are more valuable to the corporation than others. From the marketing perspective, various qualities make them more economically valuable:

- they spend more dollars on company products

- they purchase the high-margin products

- they remain as customers over longer periods of time

- they need relatively fewer inducements to remain loyal

For example, if you worked for a credit card operation, which of these customers would you find most valuable:

> *Helen is a professional with a high income and high net worth. She travels frequently for business and pleasure, charging her airline tickets, hotel bills, meals, and car rentals as she goes. Helen also keeps thousands of dollars of emergency cash on hand in the credit card company's money-market account, even though it pays only about 2.5 percent interest. She's been a cardholder with the same company for the past fifteen years and doesn't need any special discounts or inducement to stay on board. Both of her college-age children have cards on the same account.*

> *Herb has a moderate income and modest net worth. He uses his card for online purchases, shopping, and restaurant meals. Whenever he accumulates an account balance that he cannot pay off in a few months, Herb transfers his balance to whichever card company offers him a special six-month, low-interest deal. When that period expires he switches again to whichever company will offer him a special inducement.*

From a marketing perspective, Helen is a valuable customer while Herb has negative economic value. Smart marketers learn how to differentiate between people like these and target the customer segment that Helen represents, and once they capture those valuable customers, they are not reluctant to spend money on things that will keep them loyal. In their view, it's money well spent. Money spent trying to acquire and retain Herb and the segment he represents is generally wasted.

We used a credit card company as an example but could as easily have used another: a retail stock brokerage, a subscription magazine, a cell–phone service, a long–distance phone service, an Internet service provider, a bank. In each case, the old 80/20 rule applies, where 20 percent of the customers create 80 percent of the profits. Smart marketers learn to identify the profitable 20 percent segment and concentrate their customer retention efforts on them.

Chances are that you do not see the same market-oriented approach in how your company deals with its employee retention problems. Performance evaluations make it possible to identify the employees who add the most value, yet retention efforts are seldom skewed toward these high performers. True, merit bonuses are awarded and people get promotions if they do well, but salary structures seldom differ markedly between people in the same job categories (adjusted for years of service) even though their productivity levels may be very different.

In an article for the *Harvard Business Review*, Peter Cappelli highlights UPS as an example of how one company successfully differentiated between two groups of employees, with the aim of improving retention of the group with the highest value to the company.[3] In effect, the company redistributed turnover from a high–value, hard–to–replace employee segment to an employee segment that was easy to replace and train.

> *UPS recognized that drivers have some of the most important skills in the delivery business. They know the idiosyncrasies of the routes and they have direct relationships with customers. Finding, screening, and training a replacement driver are all time-consuming tasks; it may take a new hire months to learn the details of a particular route. When UPS studied the reasons its drivers left, it discovered that much of the turnover could be traced to the tedious and exhausting task of loading packages at the beginning of a run. It therefore unbundled the loading task from the drivers' job and assigned it to a new group of workers. The turnover rate for drivers fell dramatically.*
>
> *Of course, turnover in the new loading jobs averages an eye-popping 400 percent per year. But that doesn't matter. With high hourly wages and low skill requirements, the loading jobs are fairly easy for UPS to fill, typically with students or other part-timers, and fairly simple for new employees to learn.*

Tips for Recognizing High-Value Employees and Employee Segments

Managers spend so much of their time putting out fires and dealing with problems that they don't always give a lot of time and attention to determining which employees represent the greatest value to their operations. So, within your unit, make a list of the individuals who:

- provide formal or informal leadership to others,

- consistently create excellent results,

- contribute practical and valuable new ideas,

- require little or no supervision to accomplish their tasks,

- facilitate the work of others,

- have unique knowledge or skills that would be costly and time-consuming to replace, and

- could do the company great harm if they defected to direct competitors.

Managers typically give even less thought to the employee *segments* that are most essential. So think about the employee segments in your operation that:

- are essential to the operation but in short supply,

- create the most disruption when they defect,

- are most costly to recruit and train,

- control the company's link to customers and,

- act as important information transfer "nodes" within the company.

Once you've identified the individual employees and employee segments that have the highest value, be sure that they receive the lion's share of retention resources and attention.

UPS in this instance was less concerned with its overall retention rate than with the retention of particular people who were costly to replace and who added substantial value through their direct interface with customers. It identified a key employee segment and took an active step in retaining them, even though that action would make retention of a less-valued segment more difficult.

Now ask yourself:

- Which are my company's (unit's) most valuable employee segments? (See "Tips for Recognizing High-Value Employees and Employee Segments.")

- Which employee segments are least valuable and/or easily replaced and trained?

- How are our current retention efforts allocated with respect to these very different segments?

No company has an entirely free hand in how and to what degree it can allocate its retention efforts. Dramatic compensation differences between individual employees may create friction and resentment between people who must work together. Labor agreement and government regulations likewise stand in the way of some market-based approaches. Qualified retirement plan statutes, for example, do not tolerate differences in the terms of plan participation or percentage-of-compensation contributions. Nevertheless, there are strategies for keeping the best or, at a minimum, keeping them longer. We turn to these next.

Market-Based Retention Strategies

Cappelli suggests a number of practical retention strategies that recognize labor market realties and value-differences between employee segments: new compensation plans, job redesign, job customization, strengthening social ties, and hiring the less mobile. Linking potential defectors with internal job opportunities is another market-wise tool for retention.

New Compensation Plans

Most people in the know give compensation a low rating as a retention strategy. Compensation matters in the sense that you cannot recruit or retain desirable employees if they view their compensation as unfair or noncompetitive. Even people who are more dedicated to their crafts or professions than to money see their compensation as an indication of the organization's appreciation of their contributions and abilities. If they feel undervalued, they will walk. (See "Tips for Getting Compensation Right.")

Nor is compensation a reliable motivator. Years ago, Frederick Herzberg, the tribal elder of motivation, found that the incentives employers most commonly use to motivate—including pay raises—produce temporary performance improvements at best.[4]

We need only look to the "retention champions" profiled in the previous chapter to appreciate the limited utility of compensation as a motivational and retention tool. Southwest Airlines is near the bottom of the list in terms of entry-level pay within its industry (though pay relative to its competitors improves with longevity). Nevertheless, SWA employees are highly motivated to deliver on the airline's strategy, and defect at half the rate of the airline industry as a whole. Meanwhile, SAS Institute, the software company, experiences approximately one-quarter the turnover rate of its industry even though its pay scales are no higher than those of competing companies. And unlike workers in most other high-tech companies, SAS people do not receive stock options.

SWA and SAS are not unique cases. The limited value of pay as a retention tool is corroborated by various studies. Typical of these is a 1999 American Management Association/Ernst & Young workplace survey, which ranked compensation low on the scale relative to most other employee-retention factors.[5] Clearly, other strategies have greater impact on retention.

Peter Cappelli offers these pieces of advice for market-wise compensation:[6]

- Pay "hot skills" premiums to employees with crucial, rare expertise. This keeps them in place for critical periods—for

Tips for Getting Compensation Right

Compensation really matters. But as a retention issue, it's one of the easiest to address—much easier than organizational culture. Here are some strategies for getting compensation right:

Figure out what wages your industry is offering. You can do this by hiring a compensation and benefits consulting firm—or by trying these more affordable options:

- track classified ads on the Internet

- network with members of human resources organizations

- consult trade organizations

Examine internal pay disparities. Make sure that the pay for each job is roughly equivalent to that of similar jobs across the organization.

Don't assume you have to outspend your competitors. Just make sure you can meet employees' most important

example, the late design stages of a key product. Stop premiums when the skills become more available or less important to your business.

- Pay signing bonuses in stages—for example, pay out the new CEO's sign-on bonus over five years.

Job Redesign

Job redesign is another retention strategy, as the UPS example mentioned earlier makes clear. If you can identify the elements that create satisfaction and dissatisfaction within a particular job, you may be able to split off the dissatisfying tasks entirely and give them to other individuals who will appreciate the work. Outsourcing unwanted tasks is another solution, and something that every company practices to one extent or another. The big securities dealers on Wall Street, for example, don't ask their traders and clerical personnel to clean out the restrooms and vacuum the carpets before they go home at night. They outsource those tasks to commercial cleaning companies. Your company does the same.

So, if you experience unacceptable turnover in key jobs that are difficult and costly to refill, put each job under a microscope and ask:

- Which aspects of this job create employee dissatisfaction? (Ask several employees directly.)

- If we separated objectionable tasks from the job, would we need to add something else to keep it a "whole" job? And what would that something else be?

- Assuming that someone must do the objectionable tasks, what alternatives exist for handling them?

- Which is more costly to the organization, job redesign (and its consequences) or the current rate of turnover in the key job?

Psychologists Timothy Butler and James Waldroop, directors of M.B.A. career development programs at Harvard Business School, have used the term "job sculpting" to describe their own form of job design.[7] Their prescription is to design jobs that match the "deeply embedded life interests" we identified earlier in this book (application of technology, quantitative analysis, counseling and mentoring, etc.). For instance, a competent engineer with a deeply embedded life interest in counseling and mentoring might be asked to plan and manage the orientation of newly hired engineers. A salesperson with an interest in quantitative analysis might be given new duties working with the firm's market-research analysts. Effective job sculpting is only possible, however, when managers ask questions and listen carefully to what their employees tell them about their real interests.

Job Customization

Companies have almost always tried to *fit people to jobs*. Their written job descriptions and workplace routines itemize tasks and performance expectations and dictate where, when, and how the work will be performed. People are expected to conform to these what–where–how descriptions, which in reality may be highly arbitrary.

Fitting people to jobs generally fails to serve the individual employee's primary interest, which is to fit the work into his or her life situation and future plans. So when supply and demand in the labor market favors the employee, companies should think of current and potential employees as "customers" and make an effort to recognize and satisfy *their* needs. Job customization can be a powerful method through which to achieve this.

To appreciate the power of customization, consider the product and services side of the economy. In this arena, competitive markets have forced companies to provide some level of customization of the things they sell. Burger King lets customers "Have it your way." Levi's allows shoppers to customize any of its standard jeans or create unique ones from scratch. Dell, the kingpin of customizers, has pummeled its rivals with a "make-to-order" strategy for personal computers, while its competitors build and offer PCs on a take-it-as-is basis. That strategy has been a winning ticket in a highly competitive buyer's market. Customization is a powerful tool in any buyer's market—including the labor market. To customize a job to satisfy the needs of both company and employees, think about the *what, where,* and *how* of the job. The *what* can be covered through job redesign. *Where* the job is performed may involve some degree of "telework" or work from a satellite location. The *how* of work may be altered—and possibly improved—by examining specific work processes.

Strengthening Social Ties

The annals of warfare are filled with moving stories of heroism and sacrifice by individual combatants. Soldiers throwing themselves on live grenades to save their comrades. Medics crawling through withering fire to reach the wounded. Soldiers with "ticket home" wounds slipping out of field hospitals and limping back to the front line to support their buddies.

What motivates this type of selfless behavior? It's not usually "the cause," nor is it for "the Army." What motivates such heroics is more often the bond to people they know and with whom they have shared experiences. The military describes that bond as "small group cohesion." Such cohesion is powerful stuff and generally trumps any allegiance we may have the larger institution of which our small group is a part.

Small group cohesion, or "social ties," as Peter Cappelli describes this dynamic, is another strategy you can use to improve the retention of valued employees in tight talent markets. "Loyalty to companies may be disappearing," he writes, but "loyalty to colleagues is not. By encouraging the development of social ties among key employees, companies can often significantly reduce turnover among workers whose skills are in high demand."[8]

He cites the successful case of Ingage Solutions (Phoenix), which maintains a low 7 percent annual turnover among notoriously mobile software engineers by creating golf leagues, investment clubs, and softball teams. These create a social network and personal bonds between fellow employees. "Leaving the company," he points out, "means leaving your social network of company-sponsored activities."

Reconfiguring linear work processes into team-based processes can also create social ties. This was initially attempted many years ago in Sweden by Volvo, which eliminated its traditional assembly-line method of production and turned over responsibility for large chunks of assembly to teams. Nucor, whose steelworkers are the most productive in its industry, likewise organizes its production people into closely knit teams.

Hiring the Less Mobile

Cappelli's last tip for retaining people in hot labor markets is to hire from segments of that market that are just barely warm. "When people go out recruiting," he writes, "they often focus on attracting precisely those people who will be more difficult to retain. By shifting their sights to workers who can do the job but are not in high demand, organizations may be able to shelter themselves from market forces.["9] So, before you hire someone, give some extra thought to the work experience, skills, education, and native talent you *presume* a successful candidate must have. You may discover that someone with less of the above—and a person with less employment mobility—can do a credible job. This advice not only can help in retaining employees but also underscores the vital link between hiring and retention.

Reaching further down into the talent pool to fill a position may require that you do more training—which costs money—or you may have to redesign your jobs a bit. But in each case, weigh the cost of training and/or job redesign against the lower probability of turnover costs in that position. That's market-wise hiring and retention.

Tap Your Internal Labor Market

In an efficient market for talent, opportunities outside the company are bound to draw people away. Since most people are opportunity seekers, be sure that your free-ranging talent is aware of the opportunities that exist inside your own company. In a large corporation there's always a good chance that potential defectors can find what they're looking for in another operating unit or department. So make sure that internal postings are available and easy to access. One way to do this is with an online internal job search tool. Here are a few tips to observe in creating such a tool:

- Make sure that the tool's language and presentation convey the message that "it's okay to look for a new job within the company." A personal note on the site from the CEO can help here. Let people know that you want them to stay, whether in their current positions or in others.

- Make the tool fun to use. Add graphics, links to training programs, a self-assessment utility, and anecdotes about other employees who've built their careers by moving around the company.

- Personalize the tool. For example, let job seekers register one or more "personal search agents" (PSAs) that will automatically notify them via e-mail whenever a new opening of interest is posted. Allow people who are concerned with confidentiality to use a personal, noncompany e-mail address.

Summing Up

This chapter has taken a "market-driven" approach to the challenge of employee retention. Here are key points to remember:

- Not all employees have equal value to the organization; some represent greater value to the enterprise than others.

- As a manager you should identify high-value individuals *and* high-value employee segments. Scarce retention resources should be allocated to these two groups first, since high turnover in less valuable and easier-to-recruit job categories is unlikely to matter as much.

- Compensation is relevant in terms of retention, but "fair" compensation is often sufficient. You can use special compensation arrangements to address short-term issues.

- Job design, as exemplified in the UPS case, can help with retention. By identifying the elements that create satisfaction and dissatisfaction within a particular job, it is sometimes possible to split off the dissatisfying elements entirely and shift them to less critical employee segments.

- Customizing jobs, particularly for individuals and segments in high demand, can be a powerful retention tool in a hot labor market.

- The work-based social ties between individuals may indirectly strengthen an employee's commitment to their organization.

- In some cases you can improve retention by deliberately recruiting people who are in less demand, though this may result in greater training costs.

- By linking footloose employees with job opportunities within the larger organization, it may be possible to reduce organization-wide turnover rates.

Developing the Talent You Have

Strategies for Training and Development

Key Topics Covered in This Chapter

- *Why employee training and career development represent a dilemma for employers*

- *Formal and informal approaches to skill training*

- *Why training pays, with tips for reducing costs through online learning*

- *The retention benefits of career development*

- *How mentors build bonds between talented employees and their companies*

- *What to do with C performers*

T HUS FAR, we've discussed hiring techniques and various strategies for employee retention. If implemented effectively, these techniques and strategies can ensure the human assets an enterprise needs to pursue its goals effectively. Employee development is another way to fill open positions with competent people. An alternative to recruiting, it prepares people who are already a part of the organization to step into vacancies as they occur.

Employee development has several important benefits for companies. When properly managed it:

- increases the value of the company's human assets—which are *the* prime assets of companies in a growing number of industries;

- assures that competent people will be ready and able to move up as vacancies appear;

- creates a pool of individuals who understand the company and industry, and who are prepared to assume leadership as the enterprise grows; and

- contributes to effective retention.

That last point bears further elaboration. Substantial research confirms that skill and career development (the two faces of employee development) are near the top of the list of workplace features that employees favor. As the Gallup Organization concluded in a broad-based survey in 1999, "American workers who receive employer-sponsored training are more satisfied with their jobs."[1] And, as we've learned, satisfied employees are more likely to stay with you.

The Development Dilemma

Many companies consider employee development a good investment. Employees become more knowledgeable and effective, which, in turn, makes customers happier. Other companies, however, question the value of employee development in the current era of high workplace mobility. "Who," they ask, "will reap the benefit of all this expensive training and development if a) we are forced to lay these people off, or b) they leave us for jobs elsewhere?" More pointedly, they question, "Are we simply picking up the training tab for other companies—perhaps our direct competitors?"

These questions underscore a dilemma for training and career development. On the one hand, training investments make employees more valuable and more satisfied with the deal they are getting at work. This is particularly true for technology workers and engineers who recognize that their competencies erode over time. On the other hand, the same investments that make people more valuable make them more marketable and attractive to personnel poachers. Many of America's major brokerage firms, for example, have long enjoyed a reputation as great trainers of retail stockbrokers. After careful screening, they hire people with the right stuff for the business, put them through three or four months of intensive sales and investment training and licensing preparation, and then mainline them into the day-to-day work of their nationwide branch offices. Many small broker-dealers, meanwhile, spend little or nothing on training. Instead, they lie in wait for the newly trained "registered reps" to learn the ropes and build client accounts—and then they try to recruit them. It is a way to acquire good people on the cheap.

The practice of poaching workers trained by others—or "free riding"—deters some companies from investments in any training that creates transferable (as opposed to "firm-specific") skills. However, research by the Bureau of Labor Statistics indicates that the free rider problem is less a deterrent to training investments than many suppose. Over half of all companies surveyed by the BLS, including more than three-quarters of large employers, were undeterred by the free rider problem and looked to their training programs to *retain* and increase the value of their people. These respondents did not distinguish between transferable and nontransferable skills in the training programs.[2]

Indeed, most companies recognize the necessity of being a "learning organization," and that necessity appears to trump any concern with the free rider problem. Sure, every so often a competitor will lure away an individual trained at company expense. But most people will stick with companies that give them opportunities to sharpen their skills and grow in their careers. In the long run, free rider firms are the real losers because they do not invest in ongoing learning.

Skill Training

Skill training is the foundation of employee development. It has two aims:

1. to keep the skills of employees current with advancing technologies and business practices and

2. to help employees master the skills they need to advance within the company.

Skill training is a mutually beneficial arrangement. Companies that provide effective skill training gain the benefit of workers who are well versed in current standards, and employees maintain their "employability" and, in some cases, advance to higher levels.

Informal and Formal Approaches

Skill training is either informal or formal. Informal training is generally conducted through on-the-job training, or OJT. This is the least costly form of training, as it doesn't take the employee out of production. OJT is also the most prevalent approach to skill development by U.S. companies.

Generally, OJT practices in the United States are very unstructured and involve neither designated trainers nor training materials. Japanese companies, in contrast, take a more structured and planned approach to OJT since they consider it a key element of training systems that aim to develop employee competencies over long careers.[3] As described by Clair Brown and Michael Reich:

> *In Japan, OJT is as carefully planned, mapped, and recorded as company-provided classroom training. Training and skill development are an expected part of every worker's job. Each employee, from new hire to senior manager, simultaneously thinks of himself as a teacher of the person(s) below him as well as a student of the person who is above. Training the person to take your place is as important as training to move up the job ladder.*[4]

Formal training, as practiced by U.S. companies, is more highly structured than OJT and takes place in classroom or "e-learning" settings. It can be used to address both company-specific and general (transferable) skills. Formal training, however, is more expensive than OJT because it takes employees away from their work, makes use of dedicated trainers, and depends on curriculum materials that must be developed and kept up-to-date.

Formal training at many large corporations is dispensed through "corporate universities," of which there are approximately one thousand six hundred in U.S. firms. Jeanne Meister has studied these corporate institutions and points to two reasons for their popularity:[5]

- **They align employee training with business strategy.** By controlling the curriculum, the firm can focus training on the specific skills that complement its strategy. This reduces the problem of skill shortages in key positions.

- **They assure a continual upgrade of internal knowledge.** "Professional knowledge," according to Meister, "is like a carton of milk—it has a shelf life. If you're not replacing everything you know every couple of years, your career is going to turn sour."

Some firms outsource some or all of their skill training to local educational institutions, particularly vocational-technical schools. In areas where these firms are dominant employers, they often have a significant say in the curricula of these institutions—and are thus able to shape the training they need for their employees.

Skill training can not only hone key employee skills, but it can build a bond between a company and its employees. Thus it is important to assess how well your own company is meeting this need:

- Does it have a systematic and broad-based program of skill training?

- How do employees perceive the quality of that training?

- Is training clearly aligned with company requirements and strategy?

- The American Society of Training and Development has estimated that U.S. corporations spend 2 percent of payroll on employee training. Where does your firm stand relative to this average figure?

Training Pays

Investments in employee training appear to produce positive returns. A survey of three thousand businesses with twenty or more employees by the National Center on the Educational Quality of the Workforce found that companies that instituted programs that increased average employee reading or math comprehension by one grade level experienced, on average, an 8.6 percent productivity increase. Among service industries the average productivity increase was even higher.[6] And greater productivity is eventually reflected in the value of corporate equity.

Does this mean that training will produce a positive return for your company? Not necessarily. Motorola, which has extensive experience in the field of corporate training, determined that its return on training investments was highly dependent on reinforcement and unstinting management support. As described by William Wiggenhorn: "In those few plants where the work force absorbed the whole curriculum of quality tools and process skills and where senior mangers reinforced the training . . . we were getting a $33 return for every dollar spent, including the cost of wages paid while people sat in class." In contrast, Motorola plants that failed to reinforce training with follow-up meetings and a genuine emphasis on quality experienced a negative return on their investment.[7]

Online Training

Developments in the field of online training are having a major impact on formal corporate training programs. Online learning, or "distance learning," has clear advantages over formal classroom delivery of training:

- **Lower cost to supply.** Despite a high initial fixed cost in curriculum development (and ongoing expenditures for keeping learning modules current), online training is very inexpensive to deliver.

- **Elimination of travel costs and lost production time.** Sending employees off to classroom training sessions can be extremely expensive in terms of travel, lodging, and meals. Many resent the added overnights away from home. And while they are sitting in the classroom, employees aren't producing. Online learning can reduce all of these costs and drawbacks.

- **Scalable to any level of demand.** Once an online training course is produced, it can be made available to any number of employees at essentially the same cost.

- **On–demand availability.** Online training sessions are available whenever and wherever employees need them.

Despite its advantages, experts warn that online learning is seldom a complete training solution. The personal contact and

interactions that occur in classroom settings or OJT are often essential to effective learning. Ernst & Young LLP, whose training program was rated seventh in the U.S. by *Training & Development* magazine in 2002, has a very powerful computer-enabled learning
portfolio. Still, the majority of its formal learning is completed
through traditional classroom experiences. So the best solution may
be to use online training in conjunction with other formal or
informal methods of skill training.

Career Development

Career development is an umbrella term that describes the many
training experiences, work assignments, and mentoring relationships
that move people ahead in their vocations. Any company that aims
to retain its most valuable people and to fill vacancies caused by
retirements, defections, and growth from within must dedicate
resources to career development. Ultimately, it can create a strong
"bench" of people who will one day lead the company as technical
professionals, managers, and senior executives. In effect, career development is a form of "internal hiring." Also, a reputation for career
development can make the company attractive to potential recruits
who are serious about building their careers.

Career Ladders

Human resource people often refer to *career ladders* when they talk
about career development. A career ladder is a logical series of stages
that move a talented and dedicated employee through progressively
more challenging and responsible positions. For example, in the
publishing business, a person with senior editorial aspirations might
be progressively moved through various positions in production or
marketing to editorial assistant to editor. Each step would broaden
his or her skills and understanding of the business.

Formal training is generally an important element on different rungs of the career ladder. For example, an aspiring editor may need to attend a three-day course on electronic publishing and another on legal matters such as contracts and copyright rules. An R&D bench scientist being groomed for a management position in product development would benefit from course work in basic financial analysis and marketing and from personal coaching in communication and team leadership.

Some firms systematically analyze a person's current level of skills and experience and match those against the skills and experiences needed at the next step up the ladder. Gaps between what the person has and what he or she needs are then addressed through a plan that involves some combination of formal training, special assignments, and regular mentoring by a respected superior, as described in figure 5-1.

From a retention perspective, the career ladder approach is most effective when it avoids "plateaus." The employee should always feel that he or she is learning and being challenged with a manageable new set of responsibilities. There should be plenty of excitement and no opportunity of feeling "stuck" on a career plateau. That stuck feeling creates the potential for defection. If circumstances bar a promising employee's vertical advancement for the foreseeable future, his or her manager should find some type of lateral assignment that will engage the employee's interest and provide learning experiences.

FIGURE 5-1

Filling Skill and Experience Gaps

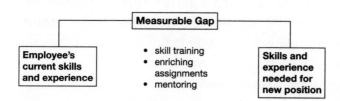

Now, ask yourself these questions about career ladders in your unit:

- What career ladders are available to your valued employees right now?

- Are they aware of those ladders and taking advantage of them?

- Have you identified and made some provisions for the skills and experiences that your charges will need to climb to the next level?

- Who, if anyone, is currently stuck on a plateau? What can be done to get them off the plateau?

As a manager, it's your responsibility to make sure that the people you value are on progressively advancing career paths. Moving ahead is good for them and increases the likelihood of their staying with your company. Their progress is also good for you since it will be easier for you to move up if you've developed a successor capable of stepping into your shoes.

Mentors

The U.S. culture applauds the self-made person. But few successful people are entirely self-made. Most successful people can point to a relative or a boss—a mentor—who helped them make the most of life's lessons and guided their professional development. Former GE CEO Jack Welch often pointed to his mother and the lessons he learned from her early in life.

A study conducted by Harvard professor Linda Hill during the late 1980s concluded that at least half of all executives had bosses who mentored them during their careers.[8] That percentage may have increased, since more and more job applicants are now inquiring about mentoring opportunities within the organizations that are recruiting them.

Hill points to three characteristics of effective mentors:

- they set high standards;

- they make themselves available to their charges; and

- they "orchestrate" developmental experiences.

Mentors who possess these characteristics play an important role in facilitating career development. And by all accounts they make a clear difference with respect to retention, perhaps because the fact of mentoring tells the employee that "We care about you and think that you are important."

Common sense tells us that mentors provide a positive bond between the employee and the firm. The strength of that bond is no doubt determined by the effectiveness of the mentor and the intensity of the mentoring relationship. And that suggests that you should assign mentors with exceptional care. In addition to Hill's three characteristics, you should also seek mentor candidates who:

- can empathize with an employee facing special challenges (for example, a female executive mentor for a female employee in a largely male organization);

- have a nurturing attitude;

- exemplify the best of the company's culture; and

- have rock-solid links to the organization. The last thing you want to do is develop a bond between a promising employee and a potential defector; nothing could sour the employee's outlook on the firm more decisively than to see his trusted counselor take a walk.

Some companies make sure that every employee has an identifiable formal mentor; others reserve mentors for upwardly mobile personnel. If your company or unit isn't making effective use of mentors in developing employee careers, consider developing a mentoring program. Begin by identifying the people who would benefit most from such a program; then, working with your own leadership group and HR, determine who would be effective and available as possible mentors.

Handling C Performers

Every organization has a distribution of performers and not every employee is promotable. At the top are the "A" performers, whose contributions are exceptional. "B" performers do very good work, while "C" performers do work that is just barely acceptable. In their study of managerial talent in two large companies, Beth Axelrod, Helen Handfield-Jones, and Ed Michaels of McKinsey & Company found that the contributions to profit growth of these groups were miles apart. On average, A managers grew profits 80 percent in one company and 130 percent in the other. C managers in these same companies achieved no profit growth whatsoever. This raised a question about where skill and career development resources should be focused. Certainly, well-managed investments in the development of A and B performers make perfect sense. But what about C performers? Should you invest in their improvement or simply move them out of the way?

Some companies regularly prune the ranks of their C-performing managers while others try to bring them up a notch. But most do nothing to deal with them. The cost of this indifference is high, both in terms of defections by good employees and lack of profit growth. As the authors write:

> Consider that every C performer fills a role and therefore blocks the advancement and development of other more talented people in an organization. At the same time, C performers usually aren't good role models, coaches, or mentors for others. Eighty percent of respondents in our survey said working for a low performer prevented them from learning, kept them from making greater contributions to the organization, and made them want to leave the company. Imagine, then, the collective impact on the talent pool and morale of a company if just 20 of its managers are underperformers and if each of them manages ten people.[9]

So, what should be done? These authors suggest a three-step approach (remember that their concern is with managerial personnel only):

- Identify C performers.

- Agree on explicit action plans for each C performer. "Certainly," they write, "some C players can improve their performance substantially if given the direction and the developmental support do so."[10] This is where the kinds of skill training we've described in this chapter may be most effective.

- Hold managers accountable for the improvement or removal of C performers.

Bradford Smart, an HR expert and consultant, likewise uses an A, B, C approach to grading employees. In his view, C players can suck the life out of an organization and should be channeled into jobs—usually at a lower level—where they have the potential to be A performers. If they fail to improve after coaching in these new positions, he feels that it is in the organization's best interest to let them go.[11]

Nevertheless, investments in C performers may be worthwhile. The only way to know for sure is to make an estimate of how organizational performance would improve if you could shift a C-level person to the next highest level. What would be the cost of doing this relative to the benefits? Is the cost less than the benefits? If the cost exceeds the benefits, then the recourse is to either move the

Tips for Career Development

- Provide a career ladder for every person you hope to retain.

- For promotable individuals, identify gaps between the skills and experience they now have and those they'll need to step into new roles. Then fill those gaps with training and appropriate assignments.

- Don't allow good people to get stuck on career plateaus.

- Make sure that everyone who needs one has a suitable mentor.

individual to a job he or she can do better, or to ask the person to leave the organization.

Summing Up

This chapter has examined the importance of employee training and career development in the hiring and retention arenas. Every organization needs to implement both training and development programs if it intends to enhance the value of its human assets and reduce the rate of defections. (See "Tips for Career Development.") If you work in a large corporation, training and development is probably the bailiwick of a specialized group of HR personnel. But don't leave it to them alone. Everyone in a management position has responsibility for enhancing the human capital assigned to them. Therefore:

- Treat the cost of employee development as an investment; it does have a real payoff, and it should reduce costs associated with the turnover of valued personnel.

- Be sure that employee development is aligned with company goals and strategy.

- Use online learning to supplement and reduce the cost of formal training.

- Map out career ladders to move talented and dedicated employees to higher levels of responsibility and performance, using formal training, mentoring, and special assignments as rungs on those ladders.

- Deal decisively with C performers. They must improve their performance (using training if necessary), move to positions where they can perform at higher levels, or leave the company.

Workplace Factors That Affect Hiring and Retention

Focusing on Culture

Key Topics Covered in This Chapter

- *Company culture, and how it can attract or repel the kinds of people you want to hire and retain*

- *Employee burnout, and how to minimize or avoid it*

- *Work-life balance, and how to make it work for both employees and the company*

H

IRING DISCUSSIONS with potential recruits almost always focus on the specifics of the job, the reporting relationships, career possibilities, and compensation and benefits. Each of these is important to job applicants. But the *climate* of the workplace may be equally important in the applicant's decision to take the job—or to stay for any length of time thereafter.

Some companies have reputations as great places to work. *Fortune* identifies the best of these companies each year in its list of the "100 Best Companies to Work For." Certain companies, such as stockbroker Edward Jones, Container Store, SAS Institute, Plante & Moran, and Frank Russell are consistently near the top of the list. *Working Mother* produces a similar "top 100" list from the perspective of women with children. The reputations of companies that make these lists undoubtedly make them more attractive to job applicants and current employees.

In this chapter, we examine three workplace factors that play an important role in hiring and retention: company culture, employee burnout, and work-life balance.

Consider Your Culture

As one of the factors that determines the attractiveness of an organization to qualified potential recruits and to current employees, culture matters. If a culture is excessively relaxed, for example, the company may have trouble attracting and retaining hard-core professionals; they may find the workplace insufficiently "serious" and detrimental to their long-term careers. If the culture is too formal and straight-laced, young and creative types are likely to feel uncomfortable and out of place. If it's unwelcoming to women and minorities, talented individuals in those communities will look for careers elsewhere. And none of these groups will be keen on working for a company if its culture is dominated by conflict, turf wars, dysfunctional senior management, or excessive hierarchical privilege.

How is your workplace culture perceived? As a first step in improving culture, ask employees these two questions:

1. Are there any important gaps between the kind of atmosphere you would like to work in and the atmosphere that currently characterizes our group? If so, what are they?

2. What measures would help improve our work culture and/or help close gaps between what we want or need and what exists?

There are many ways to close gaps between the current culture of your organization and the one you need to attract and retain great people. Here are just a few sample scenarios:

Scenario 1: Your department's young, high-energy employees want a more informal, fun, and hard-driving culture. They find the current culture too formal and rigid. In this case, you could try the following:

- Relax the dress code.
- Permit flexible schedules that let employees work long hours during high-pressure projects and more reasonable hours at other times.
- Install a ping-pong or foosball table to allow employees to burn off energy.
- Take your team to a local park for a volleyball game and picnic lunch.
- Start a tradition whereby you have a party at the end of challenging projects.

- Bring in stand-up comic videos (nothing *too* extreme, though!) and play them in a conference room during lunch.

Scenario 2: Your department has many employees with young families. They don't like the current separation between their lives at work and their lives at home. Consider these ideas:

- Institute regular family picnics—and invite people to bring their pets, too! (Many people consider their companion animals as members of the family.)
- During informal conversations, ask employees about their families—and show a genuine interest in what they say.
- Let employees bring their children to work occasionally to celebrate special occasions.
- Facilitate work from home during part of the week, or provide flextime or other arrangements to reduce family stress.
- Let employees go home early on their birthday or their wedding anniversary, or to attend parent/teacher conferences or important school events.

Scenario 3: Your group consists of researchers who want enough privacy and quiet to do the concentrated thinking and writing required by their jobs. Try these ideas:

- If your department has cubicles instead of offices with doors, invest in "white-noise" machines to drown out distracting sounds.
- Allow employees to work from home during times when they're embroiled in especially intense projects.
- Keep the frequency and length of meetings to a minimum.

But don't allow people to become too isolated. Even if they must work quietly and alone you can create a team spirit by means such as these:

- Periodically reward the group with free passes to the theater, museum exhibits, the ballet, and other cultural events.
- Start up a book or film discussion group, which could meet once a month during lunch.

Clearly, fine-tuning your culture doesn't have to be difficult or expensive. All it takes to develop an appropriate culture is a willingness to observe and listen, a little creativity, and openness to new ideas. But remember that managers must be visible symbols of the culture they aim to promote. Employees look at what top management does. If management says "Let's be casual" but still wears suits every day, anyone who aspires to being at the top will keep on wearing a suit. If management says "We care about our people" but focuses only on cost controls and dumps long-term employees at the first whiff of slowing revenues, no one will take their statements seriously. That said, by attending to your culture in these ways and really working to change it for the better, you can make your organization more attractive to the people you'd like to hire—*and* boost your retention rate.

Employee Burnout

Burnout is work exhaustion. It is sometimes self-induced, but in many other cases is a result of the workplace culture. Burnout typically manifests itself through lower job satisfaction, less commitment to the organization, and heightened intention to "do something different." In some cases, you will also see these warning signs:

- reduced self-esteem (when there's just too much to be done, some people blame themselves)

- a decline in feelings of competence and achievement

- a detached or negative approach to colleagues, customers, and clients

Burnout generally results from long-term involvement in situations that have many negative attributes, such as:

- work overload

- conflicting demands (e.g., "Think big and be creative—but don't make any mistakes")

- unclear objectives

- monotonous tasks

- interpersonal conflict

- too few real rewards (bonuses, extra time off, and so on)

- little acknowledgment of employee contributions

- failure to achieve clear success

As the list indicates, burnout is not strictly a function of the number of working hours. A person may work countless hours and still feel highly motivated. Rather, most people burn out when they feel more stress than support in their work lives.

Burnout can directly undermine your company's retention efforts—and if the organization develops a reputation as a burnout chamber, it will have trouble hiring good people. Worse, its most highly motivated employees—those who feel a strong commitment to their work—are most susceptible to burnout.

Supervisors sometimes contribute to the burnout problem without realizing it. Most supervisors have a natural tendency to load all the critical projects onto their few top performers. "I can't trust anyone else to do it right," they say in justification. And then, when these workhorses have succeeded with one project, supervisors immediately load them up with another! Meanwhile, the lax, the lazy, and the malingerers coast along, picking up their paychecks every two weeks. Are the workhorses of the department given promotions for all their good works? Not always. If they were promoted, there'd be no one left to handle the important jobs.

Consider using one of the following strategies for combating burnout: creative staffing, burnout management, and regular "re-recruitment" of top talent.

Creative Staffing

One way to avoid employee overload is to create a long-term, strategic staffing plan that ensures enough people—and enough of the right people—to do the job. Here's how:

- Get line supervisors to work closely with the human resource department and upper management to define a staffing strategy that meets department and company needs. Staffing is not entirely within the control of line supervisors—but they should do their best to clarify the human resources they need to meet their assigned goals.

- Assure that people are well trained. People who are not properly prepared for their assignments are at greater risk of burnout. So arrange for the training they need.

- Prioritize the workload. If your department is especially short-handed and unable to add people, be strategic about what you ask employees to do. Consider every task in light of whether it adds value to customers. If it doesn't add *enough* value, eliminate it. (All tasks add *some* value—be a ruthless judge of just how much.)

- Consider internal redeployment of personnel. If you don't "repot" your houseplants every so often, the roots that support them will become impacted and stop growing. The same applies to employees. Redeployment gives your organization greater flexibility while retaining top employees. Equally important, it gives employees a chance to gain new experiences and skills that may be important to them.

- Provide variety in place. Internal redeployment may not be necessary if you can find ways to vary their tasks and responsibilities. You might, for example, give one person in your department responsibility for leading a team-based project for the next six months—before rotating the task to someone else. Another person could be given temporary responsibility for facilities maintenance in your work area. Just be sure that those responsibilities are added to the individual's performance objectives and taken seriously.

In discussing redeployment or varied responsibilities with employees, be respectful of their thoughts and feelings. Rather than moving them around like chess pieces, think about what might be the best opportunities for them—and emphasize any professional development benefits offered by those opportunities. Also, redeployment should be optional. If a reassignment does take place, check with redeployed personnel periodically to see how things are going, and devise solutions to any problems that arise.

Burnout Management

Another way to avoid the high price tag of overload is for managers to actively minimize work exhaustion. Here are a few things that can be done:

- Regularly monitor workloads, especially among your top performers. One of the Big Five accounting firms did this by screening travel schedules. Individuals observed to be spending excessive time on the road or volunteering for too many projects were identified and counseled. If you find people like this, meet with them regularly to see how they're doing. This act alone can help people feel supported. And go a step further—do something about their schedules before they flame out.

- Show your appreciation for valued workers. This, too, can help outweigh some of the other negatives.

- Consider job redesign. If a valued employee shows symptoms of burnout, take a look at his or her job description. The tasks and responsibilities of the job may be beyond the powers of even an exceptional worker. In these cases, talk with the HR department and your staff about redesigning the job.

Above all, be a keen observer and a good listener. Acknowledge cries for help—such as "I don't know how to keep up," "I'm swamped," or "It looks like I'll have to work over the weekend again." Then do something to alleviate the situation.

"Re-recruit" Your Top Talent

Don't take valued employees for granted or assume that they'll want to keep working for you. Remember that the marketplace for certain skills is highly efficient and provides great mobility for top producers. Assume that you need to "re-recruit" these people from time to time. Identify your top performers and then:

- Remind yourself that high producers are your competitors' likely poaching targets.

- Show high producers how much you appreciate them—either through informal but heartfelt thanks for a job well done, small but meaningful tokens of appreciation, or in the form bonuses or extra "comp time."

Work-Life Balance

Work-life balance was one of the hottest business topics prior to the 2000–2001 recession. And despite the shock of recession-driven layoffs, it is an issue that refuses to go away. The reason that it won't is because work-life balance is a core element of employee satisfaction, loyalty, and productivity. This means that if you provide a workplace in which employees can effectively balance the requirements of work and their personal lives, retention will be less of an issue. And if you develop a reputation in the labor market as a place that supports work-life balance, you'll have an edge in hiring good people.

A study by the Ford Foundation sums up what many other researchers have found about this issue:

> *The separation of work and family undermines both business and employee goals, impairing work efficiency and family life.*
>
> *The process of challenging old assumptions and cultural beliefs that underlie work and work-family integration frees employees to think more creatively about work in general and provides companies with a strategic opportunity to achieve a more equitable, productive, and innovative workplace.*

Many of the same assumptions and beliefs that create difficulties in work-family integration also lead to unproductive work practices, undermining the companies' ability to achieve key business goals.

Restructuring the way work gets done to address work-family integration can lead to positive, "win-win" results—a more responsive work environment that takes employees' needs into account and yields significant bottom-line results.[1]

As this quotation makes very clear, work–life balance isn't just a "feel-good" issue or a perk that will cost your company money. It translates into better business performance.

In the United States, two long-term developments brought the work-life issue to a head in the late 1990s. The first was the uniquely American practice of expanding the work year, even as people became more productive and prosperous. Harvard economist Juliet Schor in her book *The Overworked American* has documented how the typical American has been asked to work more and more hours. By her count, the average U.S. work year has grown nine hours per year over the past several decades.[2] Those extra hours (and they really add up over the years) have cut directly into the time people would normally spend tending to family and personal matters. Ironic, isn't it? The more productive and prosperous Americans become, the more they are asked to work. By the late 1990s, the average American manufacturing employee was putting in 320 more hours each year than his or her counterpart in Europe.

Schor's research was completed before laptops and e-mail had made major inroads into corporate life. So you can add into her calculation of long hours the time that people now spend working at home on weekends and answering e-mails at night and during their vacations.

The result of working hours escalation: people feel squeezed. They find themselves in a winless situation in which they must either shortchange their careers or neglect their home lives. Many companies have made this situation worse by perversely buffering up-cycles in the economy with overtime. When business is booming, they ask people to work extra hours; this helps them to avoid adding new people to the payroll.

The second big contributor to the issue of work-life balance has been the growing percentage of married women in the work force. Today, well over 50 percent of married women are employed outside the home. That's good news for gender equity, but having two working spouses means that fewer people are available to keep up the household. When both are working full time and tied up in daily commutes, the time available for family and personal life takes a major hit. Meals are caught on the fly, and civic and family activities are shortchanged.

Three Principles

Work-life balance is a major issue today because so many people are saying "enough" to long days, paltry vacations, evenings spent in hotel rooms, and weekend e-mails from the boss. Many companies have gotten the message and responded with programs that help their employees balance the two sides of their lives.

At first blush, you'd think that every concession toward work-life balance would represent a cost to the sponsoring company. But as Stewart Friedman, Perry Christensen, and Jessica DeGroot explained in a widely read *Harvard Business Review* article, work-life balance can be approached from a "win-win" perspective, and not as a zero-sum game:

> *[W]e have observed that a small but growing number of managers . . . operate under the assumption that work and personal life are not competing priorities but complementary ones. In essence, they've adopted a win-win philosophy. And it appears they are right: in the cases we have studied, the new approach has yielded tangible payoffs both for organizations and for individual employees.*[3]

These researchers offer three principles for breaking through the zero-sum game:

1. **Make sure that employees understand business priorities and encourage them to be equally clear about their personal priorities.** The work of the organization must get done, and work-life balance should not be an excuse for letting it slide.

Alternatively, work cannot be an excuse for letting important personal matters slide. Friedman, Christensen, and DeGroot counsel managers to be clear about company goals and performance expectations. At the same time, they encourage employees to be clear about their goals as family members and as individuals. Once everyone's cards are on the table, schedules and assignments can usually be arranged in ways that satisfy both sides. "The fact that these managers define business success in terms of results is key," they write. "To them, outcomes matter more than process. To that end, they give their employees specific goals but also great autonomy over how to achieve those goals."[4]

2. **Recognize and support employees as "whole people" with important roles outside the workplace.** Managers can only deal with work-life conflict if they understand and show some interest in the nonworking lives of their employees. And showing a sincere interest "creates a bond and, with it, trust—which brings organizational benefits familiar to any manager."[5]

3. **Continually experiment with how work gets done.** Smart managers know that work processes must be periodically rethought and redesigned for greater efficiency and effectiveness. Work-life balance provides opportunities to experiment with these processes. In describing managers who have successfully adopted work-life balance, the authors state that "[C]onflicts between work and personal priorities can actually be catalysts for identifying work inefficiencies that might otherwise have remained hidden or intractable."[6]

Does your office have a "this is how we do things" mentality? That's bad for the company because it stands in the way of process improvement. In a dynamic environment, the best way of doing things is always changing. Flexibility is one of the ways we adapt to change and survive.

So, according to Friedman, Christensen, and DeGroot, work-life balance doesn't have to be a zero-sum game. Managed correctly, work–life balance can improve morale, increase productivity, *and* help you hire and retain the best employees. (See "Tips on Work–Life Balance.)

Telework

Many companies have found that *telework* is an effective tool for creating work–life balance. Telework describes work that is done by employees in locations other than their regular offices and is facilitated by telecommunications and Internet capabilities. The International Telework Association & Council's (ITAC) definition of telework is "using telecommunications to work wherever you need to in order to satisfy client needs: whether it be from a home office, telework center, satellite office, a client's office, an airport lounge, a hotel room, the local Starbucks, or from your office to a colleague 10 floors down in the same building."[7] The ITAC estimated that some 20 million U.S. employees were involved in some form of telework in 2001.

Proponents of telework point to measurable cost savings and benefits, including lower real estate costs, greater employee productivity, greater employee loyalty and job satisfaction, and lower personnel turnover. And the teleworkers themselves report that it helps them balance work and personal responsibilities. AT&T, which has used telework heavily since the early 1990s, conducted a random survey in 2000 of 1,238 managers and found that:

- Teleworkers put in more hours. Respondents indicated that they worked at least one hour more per day; that's equivalent to 250 hours or 6 weeks of extra (unpaid) work done by the average teleworker.

- Telework is more productive. Seventy-seven percent of AT&T's teleworkers said that they got more accomplished at home than they did in the office.

- Loyalty improves. Of those teleworkers who reported receiving competing job offers, 67 percent said that giving

Tips on Work-Life Balance

Taking our cue from the "three principles" of work-life balance described above, here are a few things you can do to make work-life balance a win–win situation:

- Give employees specific goals, but also greater autonomy over how they achieve them. Say, "You are responsible for conducting a customer survey and producing a complete report between now and mid-March. I'd like you to develop a plan for handling that."

- Give more attention to results than how, where, and when the work gets done.

- Get to know your employees and coworkers on a more personal level. Do they have civic obligations that need tending? Do they have children or aging parents to support? What hobbies or artistic pursuits absorb their attention? Do they have other skills that might benefit the company? As the Hawthorne experiments found many decades ago, making these inquiries and simply *showing an interest* in employees as individuals can have a positive impact on morale and motivation.

- Encourage people to find new and better ways of meeting their responsibilities. For example, sales managers and product development people may discover that a $5,000 investment in teleconferencing equipment could save the company $15,000 each year in travel expenses—and save each of them from weeks of unproductive travel time and many nights away from home. Supervisors may find that their 4 P.M. staff meetings—the ones that never seem to end before 6 P.M. and make everyone late for dinner—could easily be rescheduled as a lunch meeting. That would get the job done *and* get people home on time.

up the telework environment was a factor in their decision to turn down those offers.

- Attracting and retaining good employees is made easier according to 66 percent of responding AT&T managers.

- Seventy-seven percent of teleworkers are more satisfied with their careers since shifting to telework.

- Work-life balance is easier to achieve. Eighty-three percent of AT&T teleworkers reported being more satisfied with their personal and family lives since beginning telework arrangements.

AT&T also reported saving $25 million annually in real estate costs through full-time teleworkers.[8] (See "Telework Readiness.")

These remarkable findings are not unique to AT&T. But before you rush out and advocate a telework program, your company or unit should think through a number of questions, including:

- Which jobs are appropriate for telework?

- What are the legal, regulatory, insurance, and technology issues? (Individual stockbrokers, for example, cannot work from an unsupervised office of a broker-dealer.)

- How will you supervise teleworkers and assure accountability?

- Will people worry that telework will negatively affect their chances for promotions and other recognition?

Despite claims on its behalf, telework is not appropriate for every organization. In an article for the *Harvard Business Review,* Mahlon Apgar addressed this question, explaining that programs such as telework are most appropriate when companies are:

- committed to new ways of operating;

- more informational than industrial;

- dynamic, nonhierarchical, technologically advanced;

Telework Readiness

Are you a good candidate for telework? How about the people who've been asking you for permission to work from home every Friday? AT&T's telework advice site has a handy "Personnel Screener" that will evaluate the readiness of any employee for telework.[a] That automated screener evaluates telework readiness in four dimensions:

1. Prerequisites. Levels of job knowledge, experience, productivity, work quality, etc.

2. Skills. The ability to plan and manage projects, to set and reach goals, etc.

3. Work style. The ability to work with a minimum of supervision, the ability to work independently, etc.

4. Attitude factor. A willingness to try new things, a positive attitude toward telework, etc.

This self-diagnostic test helps individuals to identify their strengths as well as any barriers they might need to overcome before trying telework.

[a] See <www.att.com/telework/get_started/gs_perscr.html>.

- not command–driven; and

- willing to invest in tools and training.[9]

Telework also requires adaptation on the part of managers and supervisors. After all, their charges will not be under their watchful eyes. Who's to know if they are working or watching Seinfeld reruns? The remedy, according to most experts, is for managers to focus on results instead of activities. That means setting clear goals for individual teleworkers, making sure that they understand those goals, and setting up a system for monitoring progress in short-term stages. Managers must also find ways to integrate teleworkers into the larger group, otherwise people may become isolated and out-of-touch.

Telework clearly represents new challenges for managers, but the benefits—especially in terms of work-life balance and retention—can be substantial.

Flexible Work Schedules

Flexible scheduling is another mechanism for helping employees achieve work-life balance. Flexible scheduling allows individual employees to work something other than the usual 9-to-5, 40-hour, 5-day week. This creates opportunities for people to work even as they accommodate the needs of young children, infirm relatives, and so forth.

Many people favor flexible schedules. This is what the accounting and consulting firm Deloitte & Touche learned when it surveyed its professional staff—both men and women—in 1993. Eighty percent said that they wanted greater flexibility in where, how, and when they worked. The company responded the next year with programs for both flexible work arrangements and parental leave. By 2000, approximately nine hundred of the firm's professional employees were enrolled in one or another of these programs.[10] Did these programs help retain professional employees? Clearly so. Eighty percent of the individuals enlisted in the Deloitte & Touche programs reported that they would have left the firm if the programs had not been made available. If you figure the average replacement cost of 720 Deloitte & Touche professionals at 1.5 times annual salary (assumed here at $75,000), the savings to the firm are roughly $81 million.

Here are some typical flex-schedule arrangements used in business today:

- **Reduced-time schedules.** For example, an employee works from 10 to 5 in order to accommodate her need to drive her children to school in the morning.

- **Seasonal schedules.** For example, a tax specialist works 60-hour weeks from January through April to accommodate the tax-filing crunch, then works 30-hour weeks for the balance of the year.

- **Compressed schedules.** For example, to accommodate his weekend acting vocation, a computer technician puts in 40 hours Monday through Thursday, leaving Fridays free for rehearsals.

Flexible work schedules are appreciated by many employees. More important, they expand the pool of potential employees. If you define "who can work here" too narrowly—as 9-to-5, Monday through Friday—you automatically exclude many otherwise qualified people. Any hospital will confirm this. Desperate to recruit and retain licensed nurses, most hospitals have expanded their hiring pools through flexible scheduling. The first to do so differentiated themselves from rival institutions. You can too. But first make a business case for it.

Women as a Special Case

Everything said so far about the importance of work-life balance and its enabling mechanisms is doubled if you are having trouble hiring and retaining talented women. For reasons too numerous to discuss here, women still bear the brunt of raising and caring for young children and keeping the homestead running on an even keel—often by choice. As Felice N. Schwartz once observed, majority of women . . . are what I call career-and-family women; women who want to pursue serious careers while partic pating actively in the rearing of their children."[11] Traditional work schedules and the demands of business travel put these two goals in conflict.

It's nearly impossible to manage the household if both parents are "career primary." And it's still usually the woman who handles the home front *and* the job. This is why flex-schedules, telework, and similar programs are particularly appreciated by women. And since women represent half of the talent in the world, it makes good business sense to do what needs to be done to make their recruitment and retention as easy as possible. So, if you don't have work-life programs at your company, ask yourself:

- What is our turnover among women in key positions, and how does that compare with male turnover in the same positions?

- In exit interviews, what have defecting female employees cited as their reasons for leaving? Are they moving to firms with work-life programs?

- In our recruiting for those positions, what percentage of women versus men has rejected job offers we've made? Was work-life balance a factor in our offers being rejected?

If the answers to these questions point to clear problems in hiring and retaining women, determine through research which—if any—work-life programs would neutralize those problems. Then calculate the cost/benefit relationship of these programs.

Summing Up

This chapter examined three "workplace factors" that can affect a company's ability to attract, hire, and retain good people:

- **Company culture:** Your company culture should be appealing to the types of employees you want most to attract and retain. Depending on the types of people you are looking for, you may need to alter your culture to be more formal or informal, relaxed or fast-paced. It should also be welcoming and as free as possible from the internal conflicts that sour well-intentioned people.

- **Employee burnout:** Burnout is an important workplace factor to avoid. It can lead to lower job satisfaction, less commitment to the organization, and defections. And talented people won't be eager to work for your company if it has a reputation as a meat grinder. Watch for the several warning signs of burnout and their root causes described in this chapter. You can avoid or mitigate burnout through proper staffing, being sure that people are adequately trained and prepared for their assignments, prioritizing the workload, periodic redeployment, and/or adding variety to employee assignments.

- **Work–life balance:** Work–life balance is a core element of employee satisfaction, loyalty, and productivity. Find ways to help employees successfully manage their commitments at home and at work, and you will avoid many retention problems. And if your company develops a public reputation for providing work–life balance, its recruiters will have an edge over others in hiring good people. Telework and flexible work scheduling are the two of the most effective tools for providing work–life balance. Give them as much attention as you would other aspects of hiring and retention.

When All Else Fails

Keeping Talented Employees, Even After They Leave

Key Topics Covered in This Chapter

- *Using alumni relations and informal contacts to keep departed employees in your company's orbit*

- *The benefits of rehiring former employees*

- *Using exit interviews to uncover the root causes of employee turnover*

ONE OF THE REALITIES of market-wise retention is that you will never be able to keep all employees—particularly the most talented, who have the greatest mobility. People retire. They are "poached" by rival companies. More than a few entrepreneurial types go into business for themselves. Others simply find opportunities elsewhere that your company cannot match. Some organizations actually create employee turnover as a matter of policy. For example, CPA and law firms have "up-or-out" traditions that result in 20 to 25 percent annual turnover in their professional ranks. Perhaps one in ten employees makes partner, but all the rest have to go. One major accounting firm, in fact, admits that at any given time half of its professionals have a year or less tenure with the company *or* are within one year of leaving.

In the end, the struggle to retain good employees is a losing game. Either by death, retirement, or defection, everyone eventually leaves. The most you can hope for is to have some influence over who leaves and when.

This chapter explains how you can minimize the damage caused by employee turnover—and even benefit from it—through attention to alumni relations and the rehiring of former employees. We also explore how exit interviews can be a source for insights into improving the attractiveness of your workplace.

Keeping Valued People in Your Orbit

If you're like most managers, you hate losing a real contributor. First, there are those nagging personal questions: "Is there something wrong with me?" "Could I have done something to prevent this person's defection?" Then come thoughts about the consequences: "This won't improve my performance evaluation a bit." "Why did she have to leave right in the middle of our key project? This will really throw a wrench into the works." "How will we cover her work until we can bring someone else on board?"

Finally, you think about what you must do to fill the empty slot—and what that will cost in time and money. Talking with HR about the job description. Posting the vacancy. Scanning dozens of résumés—almost all wide of the mark. Arranging for interviews, and approving thousands of dollars for travel expenses. Then getting the new person up to speed. And all the while you know you'll be lucky to get someone as good as the person who left.

Losing a good contributor is a big headache and produces nothing but negative thoughts and extra work. But don't let those negative thoughts color your parting with the employee. In some cases you should not even use the word *parting*.

Consider the hypothetical case of Stephen, a management consultant with Global Strategy Advisors, a full-service firm. As often happens with consultants and CPAs, Stephen was lured away from his job by a client company that he had advised on marketing strategy for the past four years. That company was seeking a top-drawer professional for its vacant Vice President of Marketing post. Stephen was a logical candidate for the job and was asked by the CEO to apply. Stephen knew the company, its competitors, its industry, and industry best practices. And the company knew Stephen. Its executives and marketing staff had observed his performance over several years, and they liked what they saw. Compared with Stephen, other applicants for the VP position were simply question marks with good résumés. No one could say with any confidence how these other applicants would perform or fit in, whereas everyone agreed that Stephen was sharp and fit in nicely.

Stephen's move to the client company appeared to be a loss to his consulting firm—but was it, really? Now that he was the marketing VP of a company that made regular use of consultants, Stephen was a potential customer with a sizable budget and the authority to hire outside marketing advice. If fortune favored his career, Stephen

might rise to the CEO level, in which case he'd be hiring consultants in business strategy, mergers & acquisitions, marketing, IT, and
other areas. And as a consulting veteran, he would be in a position to
recommend different firms to both practitioners and M.B.A. graduates of his alma mater who might be seeking consulting careers.

So if Global Strategy Advisors handled its relationship with
Stephen sensibly, his defection might not be a loss after all. And if
corporate life didn't suit him, Stephen might even return to his old
firm in three or four years—and with the operating experience that
many consultants lack.

This hypothetical story is not far-fetched in the field of public
accounting and consulting. Leading firms in those industries now
have regular "alumni" programs that:

- keep track of former employees;

- maintain up-to-date, password-protected directories of former
  employees to which alumni have access;

- post job vacancies and recruiting information;

- provide free access to the firm's latest research; and

- host events that bring alumni together with current employees.

The whole point of these programs is to keep former employees
within the company's orbit, even after their official ties are severed.
That's good for business. It also makes the company more appealing
to career-minded potential recruits who understand that joining the
company makes them part of a larger network of business professionals. As Carl Stern, president and CEO of Boston Consulting
Group, put it, "I want our people to feel that in joining BCG, they
have joined a second family, and they remain part of that family for
the rest of their lives."[1]

What are you doing to maintain productive relationships with
your valued former employees? Whether you have a formal alumni
relations program or have used less formal links, keeping in touch
with departed employees can lead to new business, market intelligence, and an occasional rehiring of good people who temporarily

"got away." The effectiveness of either approach, however, will be determined by how you and your company handle departing employees. When a good employee gives notice, is he treated badly? Given the cold shoulder? Do bosses whine, "How could you leave after all we've done for you?" Those behaviors will sour the relationship forever. Instead, you should:

- congratulate the individual on his or her new career move;

- ask the HR department to help wrap up all of the departee's termination issues;

- demonstrate appreciation for his or her contributions with a party or outing;

- plan to communicate with the departee in a month or two to see how he or she is doing; and

- keep him or her posted on employment opportunities within the company.

Hiring Former Employees

Thomas Wolfe's message that you can't go home again does not hold true for former employees. Just because a valued person has left your company, don't assume that he or she is gone for good. Some women drop out while their children are infants but are ready to return a few years later. Others leave for what appear to be great career moves, only to be disappointed and disillusioned.

Rehires can be a valuable asset for your company. First, they know your business and how to get things done there. This gives them a huge advantage over people hired from the outside, who generally need many months to learn the ropes and become effective. Second, rehires return with broader experience and, in many cases, new skills. Finally, every returning defector sends a loud and clear message to others that the grass isn't greener elsewhere.

There are few statistics on the number of employee rehires, or "boomerangs" as they are sometimes called. For example, in 2000, the accounting firm of Ernst & Young claimed on its Web site that nearly 25 percent of its customer-serving new hires in North America were former employees. During the following year—when most companies weren't hiring anyone—Ernst & Young made a special effort to re-recruit good IT employees who had defected to now-defunct dot-com companies. It even set up a national Alumni Relations Office to manage this important aspect of its human resource business.[2]

Here are a few things you can do to increase the number of employee rehires:

- Cure the problems that made them leave in the first place. Exit interviews and direct investigation are the best ways to determine the root causes of defection. If you find that a bad regional manager has been driving his most capable sales people away, replace that manager—and then invite the best of the defectors to return.

- Keep the lines of communication open between your firm and the best of its departed employees. Use some of the alumni relations tactics cited above. Communicate with them periodically, ask about how they're doing in their new jobs, and keep them up to date concerning job openings at your company.

- Make re-employment as easy as possible. There's a certain amount of discomfort involved with returning to one's old company. Eliminate that discomfort through public statements that "Our door is always open to valued former employees." Celebrate each return, just as you would the return of a former customer. "We're glad you're back!"

Perhaps the biggest and most celebrated rehire in recent memory was Apple Computer's rehiring of departed founder Steve Jobs. Jobs returned to his former post older, more experienced, and undoubtedly wiser, and his return marked the beginning of an important revitalization for the then-beleaguered company.

It's unlikely that any one of your rehires will have the impact that Steve Jobs had on Apple, but you'll know a great deal about the person you're getting, and the hiring outcome is more likely to be more successful than if you hired an unknown off the street.

Exit Interviews

Most HR departments conduct exit interviews with departing employees, either directly or through questionnaires. The aim of these interviews is to get feedback about the firm, its operations, the root causes of turnover, and the performance of its managers from people who now have less reason to hedge or conceal their views.

If your company isn't doing this—or not doing it in a serious or systematic way—insist on a change. At a minimum, an exit interview should seek answers to these questions:

- What originally attracted you to this company?

- How satisfied were you with employment here (on a 1-5 scale)?

- How would you assess your boss or supervisor (again, on a 1-5 scale on various dimensions: ability to communicate, leadership, fairness, employee development, etc.)?

- Why are you leaving? (if the exit is voluntary)

- Would you consider applying for another job here in the future?

- How could we make this a better place to work?

The responses gathered through many exit interviews can help you identify the root causes of turnover and build a solid strategy for improved retention. In this sense, information gleaned from exit interviews is an important part of continuous workplace improvement. Chances are your company seeks the root causes of below-standard output elsewhere in the organization—on the production floor, in customer service levels, and so forth—with a goal to improve process quality. What departing employees tell you should be used in the same way.

Summing Up

Acknowledging that employee turnover is inevitable, this chapter has offered three ways to potentially benefit from departing employees:

- Keep up contact and good relationships with company alumni; doing so can sometimes provide your company with new business, market intelligence, and, in some cases, rehires.

- View highly valued former employees as potential rehires; in most cases, a former employee returns with broader experience and new skills—both of which can benefit your company.

- Use exit interviews to obtain as much information as possible about the root causes of employee turnover.

Sample Job Description

A job description is a profile of a particular job, its essential functions, reporting relationships, hours, and required credentials. It identifies what the job-seeker agrees to do in return for pay and benefits. Rather than focusing on how an employee should spend his or her time, a good job description should focus on performance and the *results* the company expects in the bargain. What will success look like? How will it be measured? How should the employee's work affect the mission and needs of the company? It is also an attempt to describe the qualifications needed to perform the job.

The sample represented below contains the basic elements you should include in job descriptions you develop.

Should you reveal the salary range in the job description? Many employers are reluctant to do this because of fear of offending existing employees, preferring to veil uneven hiring practices. This is not only bad management, in the United States it is also potentially illegal if it indicates that you are not offering equal pay for equal work.

For your convenience, you can use the "Job Profile" form to develop job descriptions for your open positions.

Job Profile

Position Title: Secretary II

Salary Grade: 6

Required/Preferred Experience, Skills: 2–3 years of secretarial experience required; word processing and spreadsheet experience required, preferably with MS Word 2000 and MS Excel 5.0. Good communication skills and ability to work on a project team are essential; 80 wpm typing required.

Education: Post–high school business or secretarial training required; some college preferred.

Essential Functions: Essential functions include, but are not limited to:

- Typing and proofreading correspondence, memoranda, and reports

- Organizing and maintaining departmental files

- Entering data into spreadsheet files

- Answering telephone and arranging appointments for sales personnel

Other Functions: Contributes to departmental goals by accomplishing related duties as required.

Salary range: $20,000–$25,000

Targeted Interview Questions

This appendix offers a bank of interview questions you can use to extract the information you need from job applicants. Remember that you cannot make a good hiring decision without good and sufficient information about the applicant. And a bad decision will cost you and your company plenty. The questions are arranged according to category.

Introduction

What attracted you to our company (this position)?

How did you hear about the job opening?

Learn about a Candidate's Current or Most Recent Job

How did you get your present job?

What are (were) your areas of responsibility?

Describe a typical day in your current (most recent) position.

What do you find most satisfying about the job? Why?

What do you find most frustrating about the job? Why? How do you deal with these frustrations?

What is the most challenging aspect of your position? Why?

What have you learned most from the job? How has that contributed to your growth?

If we were to ask your present employer about your abilities, what would she or he say?

How would your direct reports describe you? Your peers?

What would your current or most recent manager say your greatest contribution has been?

Work Experience

How has your work experience prepared you for this job?

Describe for me one or two of your greatest accomplishments and biggest disappointments.

What has been the most significant challenge you have managed? How did you manage it?

What is the most creative achievement you have experienced at work?

What can you say about yourself that has contributed to your success?

Can you tell me about a new initiative or procedure you have worked on that had a positive impact?

Give me two examples of good decisions and two examples of poor decisions you have made in your work life.

Describe a time when your job performance fell short of expectations.

What qualities can you bring to this position?

Give me an example of your ability to supervise others.

Assess a Candidate's Skills

Do you consider yourself a self-starter? If so, explain why. Give examples.

What is your greatest strength that would benefit our organization?

How have you positively influenced others to get a job done?

Describe a decision that you made when you did not have all the pertinent information.

Tell me about a time you made a decision quickly.

How have you supported a new policy or procedure with which you have disagreed?

In what ways do you motivate your direct reports? Your peers?

Describe a situation when you had to seek out information, analyze it, and make a decision.

Describe a recent high-risk decision that you made. How did you make this decision?

Assess a Candidate's Style

Of all the jobs you have had, which did you like the most? Why?

How have you preferred to be supervised in your previous jobs?

What role have your past supervisors played in supporting you in your job? Your career?

What type of organization do you prefer to work for?

Do you prefer working in groups or alone?

Describe a work group experience that you found rewarding.

What qualities do you value in your supervisor?

In what types of environments do you feel most effective?

How much direction and feedback do you need to be successful?

What is most exciting to you about change? What is most frustrating about it?

How have you dealt with organizational changes?

How would you describe yourself as a supervisor?

How would your supervisor describe you?

What was the most difficult management decision you've ever had to make?

What kinds of people do you like to work with?

What type of person do you find it most difficult to work with? Why?

What things frustrate you the most at work? How do you cope with them?

Career Aspirations and Goals

What are some of the things you would like to avoid in your next job? Why?

Why are you leaving your present job?

How does this job fit into your overall career plans?

Where do you see yourself three years from now?

How have your career aspirations changed over the years? Why?

What would you most like to accomplish if you got this job?

Education

What special aspects of your education, experience, or training have prepared you for this job?

In what areas would you most need (like) additional training if you got this job?

What aspects of your education or training will be useful for this job?

What are your educational goals?

Customer Service

Describe a time when you worked to meet a customer's needs. What were the customer's needs? How did you assist the customer? What actions did you take and what was the outcome?

Self–Control

Describe a time when you dealt with a particularly stressful situation or with a hostile colleague or customer. What was the situation? What actions did you take? What did you say? What was the response or reaction?

Critical Thinking

Tell me about a time when you had to evaluate a situation in order to resolve a problem. What was the situation? What actions did you take? What was the outcome? How did you know you were successful?

Results Orientation

Describe a time when you took the initiative to improve how you worked or how something operated (a process, system, team). What led to the situation? What actions did you take? What was the outcome? How did you know your solution was an improvement?

Closing

Are there any additional aspects of your qualifications that we have not covered that would be relevant to the position we are discussing? What questions do you have about our organization?

Legal Landmines in Hiring

Note: This appendix applies to U.S. hiring situations only.

Employment in the United States is governed by many laws on hiring, firing, discrimination, sexual harassment, benefits and pension, and union activities, to name just a few. Hiring discrimination laws protect job applicants from questions that are not directly related to the applicant's ability to do the job.

The relevant laws applying to hiring are:

- The Civil Rights Act of 1964, which forbids the use of arbitrary and artificial requirements that would create de facto barriers to employment because of a person's race, gender, national origin, ethnicity, or religion.

- The Age Discrimination in Employment Act, which prohibits workplace discrimination against persons of forty years and older.

- The Pregnancy Discrimination Act of 1978, which forbids workplace discrimination on the basis of pregnancy or a related medical problem.

- The Americans with Disabilities Act of 1990 (ADA), which forbids discrimination against physically and mentally disabled people.

- The Immigration Reform and Control Act of 1986, which forbids discrimination against individuals based on national origin and citizenship.

This appendix offers suggestions on how you, as a job interviewer, can obtain the information you need while remaining on the right side of these various laws. It is by no means complete, nor is it intended as a source of legal advice. It's only purpose is to alert you to aspects of the hiring process where care must be exercised.

When hiring, there are some questions you cannot ask without fear of legal liability. HR departments are knowledgeable about these questions and make sure that none appear on job application forms. Questions prohibited on these forms are also prohibited during job interviews. Here are the areas where you must either *not* ask questions or observe great care:

- **Age or date of birth.** This could run you afoul of the Age Discrimination in Employment Act. However, certain public safety positions have age limits for hiring. Questions about age may be asked if necessary to satisfy provisions of state or federal law. For example, you *can* ask, "If hired, can you show proof that you are at least 18 years old?" You will need the actual age and date of birth to comply with benefits and other company plans; however, these can only be obtained *after* the individual is hired.

  Other age-related *illegal* questions include: "How soon do you plan to retire?" "Can you work for a younger manager?" "Do you think you could keep up with the rest of the younger employees?"

- **The applicant's religion.** No inquires on this subject may be asked except by religious organizations as provided by certain statutes. Nor may you inquire about the following: "Do you intend to take time off for your religious holidays?" "Do you have any unusual religious practices that we should be aware of?" "Do you think you can fit into our mostly (fill in the religion) department?"

  It is appropriate to ask, "This position requires weekend work (travel). Do you have any responsibilities that conflict with these requirements?

- **Marital status.** Never ask if the applicant is single or married. Also, avoid any question that would be construed as an indirect attempt to determine marital status, such as, "What does your husband/wife do for a living?"

- **Intention to have children.** This is another forbidden area. Do not ask "Do you have children?" "Do you intend to have children?" Indirect questions in this area are also off-limits, such as, "What child-care arrangement would you have to make if you took this job?"

- **Race.** Never ask the applicant about his/her race or ethnicity. Nor can you require an individual to submit a photograph with his or her job application or résumé.

- **Gender or sexual orientation.** Another off-limits area.

- **National origin, ethnicity, and/or ancestry.** Do not ask any questions about these; nor may you inquire about the national origins of the applicant's parents, spouse, or other close relatives. And don't make the innocent mistake of saying, "Draculaskov is an interesting last name. What kind of name is that?" Other question not to ask are: "Do you speak English at home?" "Will you wear American clothes or your native dress to work?"

- **Citizenship.** You may *not* ask "Are you a U.S. citizen." Nor may you inquire into the citizenship of the applicant's parents or spouse. However, you may ask "Are you legally authorized to work in the United States?" Or, "If hired, can you show proof of your eligibility to work in the United States?"

- **Disability or handicap.** Make no inquiry whether the applicant has a physical or mental disability or handicap or about the nature or severity of either. The same applies to questions about alcoholism, drug addition, and AIDS. Other illegal questions include: "Are you taking any medications?" "Do you have frequent doctor appointments?" "Have you ever been hospitalized or received workers' compensation?"

You may, however, ask, "Are you able to perform the essential functions of this job with or without reasonable accommodation?"

- **Education.** Make no inquiry unless educational background is demonstrably related to the ability to do the job. For example, someone applying for a position as a financial analyst must meet certain educational requirements in mathematics, finance, and statistics; a mail room employee would not. However, avoid questions designed to determine the age of the applicant.

- **Arrests and conviction records.** Unless the person is applying for a security-sensitive job, you cannot ask about these.

- **Garnishment of wages.** Never ask, "Are your wages being garnished?"

If there is any simple advice in this maze of "don't ask" categories it is this: if your question does not relate *directly* to the job at hand, don't ask it.

Notes

Introduction

1. For the cost of "mis-hires," see Bradford D. Smith, *Topgrading* (New York: Prentice Hall Press, 1999), 45–59.

Chapter 1

1. Based on "21st-Century Job Descriptions," *Harvard Management Communication Letter* (February 2001): 10–11.

2. Pierre Mornell, *Hiring Smart!* (Berkeley, CA: Ten Speed Press, 1998), 123.

3. Ibid., 124

Chapter 2

1. This section draws heavily on "Online Hiring? Do It Right," *Harvard Management Update*, February 2000.

2. Peter Cappelli, "Making the Most of On-Line Recruiting," *Harvard Business Review* 79, no. 3 (March 2001): 139–146.

3. Claudio Fernández-Aráoz, "Hiring Without Firing," *Harvard Business Review* 77, no. 4 (July–August 1999): 108–120.

4. Ibid.,114.

5. Ibid., 114–115.

6. See Melissa Raffoni, "Use Case Interviewing to Improve Your Hiring," *Harvard Management Update*, July 1999.

7. Ibid.

8. Timothy Butler and James Waldroop, "Job Sculpting: The Art of Retaining Your Best People," *Harvard Business Review* 77, no. 5 (September–October 1999): 144–152.

9. Ibid., 144–152.

10. Subrata Chakravarty, "A Model of Superb Management: Hit 'Em Hardest with the Mostest," *Forbes,* 16 September 1991: 48-51.

11. As told in Dwight Gertz and João P.A. Baptista, *Grow to Be Great* (New York: The Free Press, 1995), 154–155.

12. Material in this section is drawn from Edward Prewitt, "Personality Tests in Hiring: How to Do It Right," *Harvard Management Update,* October 1998.

13. All quotes from Tom Norton are cited in Prewitt.

14. Ibid.

Chapter 3

1. "Commitment in the Workplace: The 1999 Employee Relationship Report Benchmark Study," Hudson Institute/Walker Information.

2. Anthony J. Rucci, Steven P. Kirn, and Richard T. Quinn, "The Employee-Customer-Profit Chain at Sears," *Harvard Business Review* 76, no. 1 (January–February 1998): 83–97.

3. Dave Ulrich, Richard Halbrook, Dave Meder, Mark Stuchlik, and Steve Thorpe, "Employee and Customer Attachment: Synergies for Competitive Advantage," *Human Resource Planning* 14, no. 2 (June 1991): 89–103.

4. "Attraction and Retention from Employee Perspectives," William M. Mercer, Internal Report, April 1998.

5. "How to Keep Your 50-Somethings," *Harvard Management Update,* September 1999.

6. Kristen B. Donahue, "Why Women Leave—And What Corporations Can Do About It," *Harvard Management Update,* June 1998.

7. Ed Michaels, Helen Handfield-Jones, and Beth Axelrod, *The War for Talent* (Boston, MA: Harvard Business School Press, 2001), 47.

8. Charles Fishman, "Sanity, Inc.," *Fast Company,* January 1999, 87.

Chapter 4

1. Peter Cappelli, "A Market-Driven Approach to Retaining Talent," *Harvard Business Review* 78, no. 1 (January–February 2000): 103–111.

2. The application of customer retention concepts to the problem of employee retention has been articulated in an unpublished work by Robert Duboff, *Hobson's Solution: Putting People and Customers First,* Ernst & Young, LLP, 2001. In it, Duboff advises companies to begin looking at their employees as customers. Doing so, he believes, makes it possible to apply proven marketing concepts to the task of identifying and retaining the most valuable employees and employee segments.

3. Ibid., 107.

4. See Frederick Herzberg, "One More Time: How Do You Motivate Employees?" *Harvard Business Review* 65, no. 5 (September–October 1987): 109–120.

5. American Management Association/Ernst & Young Survey press release, Ernst & Young, LLP, 20 April 1999.

6. Cappelli, "A Market-Driven Approach to Retaining Talent," 105–106.

7. Timothy Butler and James Waldroop, "Job Sculpting: The Art of Retaining Your Best People," *Harvard Business Review* 77, no. 5 (September–October 1999): 144–152.

8. Cappelli, "A Market-Driven Approach to Retaining Talent," 108.

9. Ibid., 109.

Chapter 5

1. The Gallup Organization, *Employees Speak Out on Job Training: Findings of a New Nationwide Study*, 1999.

2. U.S. Bureau of Labor Statistics, "BLS Reports on Employer-Provided Formal Training," press release, 23 September 1994.

3. Clair Brown and Michael Reich, "Developing Skills through Career Ladders: Lessons from Japanese and U.S. Companies, *California Management Review* 39, no. 2 (Winter 1997): 124–125.

4. Ibid., 129.

5. "Corporate Universities: The New Pioneers of Management Education: An Interview with Jeanne Meister," *Harvard Management Update,* October 1999.

6. See Edward E. Gordon, "Investing in Human Capital: The Case for Measuring Training ROI," *Corporate University Review,* January-February 1997.

7. William Wiggenhorn, "Motorola U: When Training Becomes an Education," *Harvard Business Review* 68, no. 4 (July–August 1990): 75.

8. Linda A. Hill, *Becoming a Manager* (Boston, MA: Harvard Business School Press, 1992), 218.

9. Beth Axelrod, Helen Handfield-Jones, and Ed Michaels, "A New Game Plan for C Players," *Harvard Business Review* 80, no. 1 (January 2002): 83.

10. Ibid., 85.

11. Hank Gilman and Lori Ioannou, "The Smart Way to Hire Superstars," *Fortune,* 10 July 2000, online edition, <www.fortune.com>.

Chapter 6

1. Rhona Rapaport and Lotte Bailyn, "Rethinking Life and Work," The Ford Foundation, <www.fordfound.org>.

2. Juliet Schor, *The Overworked American* (New York: Basic Books, 1998), 12.

3. Stewart D. Friedman, Perry Christensen, and Jessica DeGroot, "Work and Life: The End of the Zero Sum Game," *Harvard Business Review* 76, no. 6 (November–December 1998): 119–129.

4. Ibid., 121.

5. Ibid., 122.

6. Ibid., 124.

7. See the ITAC web site at <http://www.telecommute.org> for its definition of telework and its most recent research findings.

8. See <http://www.att.com/telework> for AT&T's most recent research on telework. The site also includes many articles on this subject as well as a "getting started" guide to implementing telework programs and policies.

9. Mahlon Apgar IV, "The Alternative Workplace: Changing Where and How People Work," *Harvard Business Review* 76, no. 3 (May–June, 1998): 121–136.

10. See <http://www.deloitte.com/more/women/wiar/movie.html>.

11. Felice N. Schwartz, "Management Women and the New Facts of Life," *Harvard Business Review* 67, no. 1 (January–February, 1989): 65–76.

Chapter 7

1. See BCG's Web site, <https://www.bcg.com/alumni/alumni_login.asp>, 22 February 2002.

2. "Alumni Relations During a Downturn," *Daily Deal,* 27 September 2001.

Glossary

AFFILIATION The opportunity to work with liked, admired, and respected colleagues; a work value that many employees consider important.

ALUMNI RELATIONS An organized program that aims to maintain positive links between the firm and former employees.

ATTRITION The departure of employees.

BOOMERANG A former employee who is rehired.

BURNOUT Work exhaustion resulting from overload or other changes in an employee's work situation.

CONTINGENT WORK FORCE The portion of the work force consisting of part-time employees, freelancers, and temporary workers.

DEMOGRAPHIC CHANGE Change in the makeup of a population (for example, age, gender, or racial proportions).

DIVERSITY Variation in age, gender, race, ethnicity, sexual orientation, physical ability, and other characteristics in the work force.

FREE AGENCY Self-employment, in which workers serve various clients on a temporary, contractual basis.

GEN-XERS Twenty- to thirty-year-old employees; a term used most commonly in the United States.

INTELLECTUAL CAPITAL The knowledge and skills of employees that create value for the organization.

JOB DESCRIPTION A profile of a job, its essential functions, reporting relationships, hours, and required credentials.

JOB SCULPTING   Reshaping an employee's current role so that the individual is able to express his or her core business interests, do the work he or she values most, and use or learn the skills that he or she wants to develop.

MACROCULTURE   A company's overall atmosphere, values, and manners of interpersonal interaction.

MICROCULTURE   The atmosphere, values, and manners of interpersonal interaction that characterize a division, department, or team.

RETENTION   Keeping talented employees on the work force.

TURNOVER   The change in a company's work force as employees leave and new hires arrive. Turnover is the sum of voluntary and involuntary separations.

WORK-LIFE BALANCE   The opportunity for employees to devote adequate time to both work and nonwork matters in their lives.

For Further Reading

Cultural Fit

Harris, Jim and Joan Brannick. *Finding and Keeping Great Employees.* New York: AMACOM, 1999. This book focuses on corporate cultures—knowing what your company's culture is, developing it, communicating it, using it to retain people. Includes two chapters on retention best practices, offering both principles ("engage the soul") and real-world examples (for example, Timberland lets employees donate up to forty hours a year to outside projects).

Roth, Daniel. "My Job at The Container Store," *Fortune*, 10 January 2000. Want an inside look at how culture can keep employees? This article gives you a behind-the-scenes glimpse at what it's like to work at The Container Store—named the best company to work for in the United States.

Stauffer, David. "Cultural Fit: Why Hiring Good People Is No Longer Good Enough," *Harvard Management Update*, March 1998. Searches for good candidates are becoming more expensive and more difficult for HR departments in companies of all sizes. With the tempting option to settle for a "near fit," most professionals warn that finding someone who is the correct match for the firm's culture and values is at least as important as finding someone with the correct skill set. The article also offers some suggestions for handling the search process.

Cost of Turnover

A Web site operated by the University of Wisconsin-Cooperative Extension provides a handy cost-of-turnover calculator that allows you to input your company-specific cost data and quickly determine turnover cost per defector. See http://www.uwex.edu/ces/cced/publicat/turn.html. Another can be found at http://www.advantagehiring.com/calculators/ahi_calc_turnover.htm.

Kaye, Beverly and Sharon Jordan-Evans. "Retention: Tag, You're It!" *Training & Development,* April 2000. In this article, the authors explain the true costs of losing a valued employee and show you how to diagnose— and close—gaps between your desired and actual retention goals. Includes tips on building a retention task force.

General

"Finding—and Keeping—Good Young Employees," *Harvard Management Update,* October 1999. The number of workers aged 25 to 34 has declined by about 12 percent since 1990 and will continue to fall for several more years. To cope with this shortage, some companies focus on new recruitment strategies, outsource or automate jobs once done by entry-level employees, or hire people they once wouldn't have considered. But consultants in the field say there's also an opportunity here to reinvent what constitutes both a job and a workplace. HMU asked the experts for tips on determining the right combination of strategies for solving your company's staffing problems.

Smart, Bradford. *Topgrading: How Leading Companies Win By Hiring, Coaching, and Keeping the Best People.* New York: Prentice-Hall Press, 1999. Smart reveals his approach to intensive investigation of key job applicants.

Hiring

Adams, Bob and Peter Veruki. *Streetwise Hiring of Top Performers.* Holbrook, MA: Adams Media Corporation, 1997. The authors have compiled an extensive list of interview questions, annotated to indicate how they can be useful to the interviewer. There are also several chapters describing the interview process itself.

Mornell, Pierre, Dr. *45 Effective Ways for Hiring Smart! How to Predict Winners & Losers in the Incredibly Expensive People-Reading Game.* Berkeley, CA: Ten Speed Press, 1998. Presents strategies for measuring candidates, emphasizing behavior, not words. Covers all stages of the hiring process from pre-interview screening to interviewing to checking references and background.

Roberts, Michael J. "Note on the Hiring and Selection Process," Harvard Business School Case Note, #9-393-093, 1993. Describes a model for thinking about the hiring and selection process.

Swan, William S. *Swan's How to Pick the Right People Program.* New York: John Wiley & Sons, Inc., 1989. Provides a field-tested and systematic approach to choosing the best candidates.

Interviewing

Falcone, Paul. *96 Great Interview Questions to Ask before You Hire.* New York: AMACOM, 1997. This book provides a collection of interview questions with notes about how to use them and how to follow up. The questions are categorized by purpose and by type of job candidate.

Hattersley, Michael. "Conducting a Great Job Interview," *Harvard Management Update,* March 1997. This article focuses on how to get beyond the "pat" question-and-answer formula of the well-prepared interview candidate.

Kanter, Arnold B. *The Essential Book of Interviewing.* New York: Random House, 1995. Kanter's book gives interviewers and interviewees the techniques to master the interview process. He explains how to prepare for an interview, ask the right questions and avoid the wrong ones, and make decisions.

Recruiting

"Online Hiring? Do It Right," *Harvard Management Update,* February 2000. Managers can find new employees through the Web—but not just by posting job openings. The Web allows managers to reach larger numbers of potential candidates, in venues that weren't available in the past. It also allows companies to pinpoint their recruiting efforts and to set themselves apart from competitors through creative electronic tactics. This article offers some guidelines, and a sidebar entitled "Keep Web Hiring in Perspective" describes the negative aspects of online hiring.

Cappelli, Peter. "Making the Most of On-Line Recruiting," *Harvard Business Review* 79, no. 3 (March 2001): 139–146. This article examines hiring right through the lens of recruiting technology, showing how it lets companies find, attract, and screen candidates.

Retention

The Center for Organizational Research. *A Research Report on the Brave New World of Recruiting and Retention: Facts, Trends, Practices, and Strategies.* Lexington, MA: Linkage, Inc., 2000. This article shows managers how to implement a key retention strategy: helping employees redefine their current roles so that the work better matches their core business interests, work reward values, and skills.

Dobbs, Kevin. "Winning the Retention Game," *Training,* September 1999. In this selection, Dobbs affirms the importance of designing unique, creative strategies for retention—emphasizing that "one-size-fits-all" approaches no longer work. He outlines the new rules driving turnover patterns and provides tips for combating attrition through creative perks.

O'Reilly, Charles and Jeffrey Pfeffer, "Southwest Airlines: Using Human Resources for Competitive Advantage (A)," Case HR1A. Stanford: Stanford University Graduate School of Business, 1995. This case study provides a revealing inside look at the work environment at SWA and the features that make its employees loyal and customer-directed.

Training and Career Development

Cappelli, Peter. *The New Deal At Work: Managing the Market-Driven Workforce*. Boston: Harvard Business School Press, 1997. The author brings his "market-driven" approach to human resources to a very good section on the dilemma that employers created when they broke the traditional unwritten contract with their employees. The free agency climate that resulted has made training and career development risky. He explains how some firms have responded by asking employees to pay for their own training, for example, or take responsibility for reimbursing training costs if they defect within certain time periods.

Olesen, Margaret. "What Makes Employees Stay," *Training & Development*, October 1999. Investing in training can help employees move forward in their professional development—and gives your firm a major competitive edge in the war for talent. This article explores the impact of training on retention and includes tips and three case studies.

Work–Life Balance

For companies considering a telework program, the International Telework Association & Council (ITAC) offers its "e-Work Guide: How to Make Telework Work for Your Organization." The 100-page guide ($99) consists of recommended practices from telework experts. Check it out at www.telecommute.org/brp/ework_guide.shtml.

AT&T likewise has lots of information on getting started in telework. It also sells consulting services to companies that want to set up programs. Its site, www.att.com/telework/get_started, has information for employees, managers, and companies on this subject.

Moore, Jo-Ellen. "Are You Burning Out Valuable Resources?" *HR Magazine*, January 1999. Burnout from work exhaustion is a main reason that people leave their jobs. This articles shows you what burnout looks like, who's most susceptible (your top performers!), and how you can manage exhausted employees.

Index

About the Subject Adviser

Peter Cappelli is the George W. Taylor Professor of Management at The Wharton School and Director of Wharton's Center for Human Resources. He is also a Research Associate at the National Bureau of Economic Research in Cambridge, MA, and a member of the executive committee of the National Center on Post-Secondary Improvement for the U.S. Department of Education at Stanford University. He has degrees in industrial relations from Cornell University and in labor economics from Oxford, where he was a Fulbright Scholar. He has been a Guest Scholar at the Brookings Institution, a German Marshall Fund Fellow, and a faculty member at MIT, the University of Illinois, and the University of California at Berkeley, as well as The Wharton School. He was a staff member on the Secretary of Labor's Commission on Workforce Quality and Labor Market Efficiency from 1988–90 and was recently named by Vault.com as one the twenty-five most important people working in the area of human capital.

Professor Cappelli's research has examined changes in the workplace and their effects on employers. His publications include *Change at Work* (Oxford University Press, 1997), a major study for the National Planning Association on the restructuring of U.S. industry and its effects on employees, and *The New Deal at Work: Managing the Market-Driven Workforce* (Harvard Business School Press, 1999), which examines the challenges associated with the decline in lifetime employment relationships. His recent work on managing retention and on new approaches to recruiting appears in the *Harvard Business Review.*

About the Writer

Richard Luecke is the writer of several books in the Harvard Business Essentials series. Based in Salem, Massachusetts, Mr. Luecke has authored or developed over thirty books and dozens of articles on a wide range of business subjects. He has an M.B.A. from the University of St. Thomas.